Alan Heeks is a classic baby boomer, born in 1948. He gladly admits to being an ageing hippie, who studied English at Oxford in the Sixties, and made it to Haight-Ashbury and Chicago in 1968. He also has a Harvard MBA, and a successful business management career. At age 42, Alan gave back the company Jaguar and dropped out of the corporate world.

Alan describes his midlife period as several years of shipwrecks and slowly reinventing himself. This included creating a woodland retreat centre, divorce and depression, blind dates, and studying with spiritual teachers.

Since turning 60, Alan has remarried and settled in West Dorset, near the sea. His current loves include writing, gardening, music, grandchildren, and slowing down in nature.

* * *

Praise for *Not Fade Away*:

Practical, informative and friendly. If you are over sixty but still feel alive and up for it, then Alan Heeks gives us some really useful hints and resources. Money. Relationships. Sex. Family. Work. It's all in here – with good advice and ideas. Recommended for all of us who won't just fade away! —

William Bloom, author of *Feeling Safe:*
How to be Strong and Positive in a Changing World

Alan is passionately engaged in the exploration of the ageing process and the sometimes hidden gifts therein. He brings a wealth of experience and a lifetime dedicated to playing his part in making the world a better place. A thoughtful and inspiring book.

Malcolm Stern, co-founder and co-director of Alternatives at
St James's Piccadilly, author and leading UK psychotherapist

Harvesting the fruits of a life lived to the full, Alan Heeks has given us a book of great insight and practical value. Gentle, compassionate, and wise, Not Fade Away *is also forthright, brave, and challenging. Brimming with quiet humour and questions that prise away the fearful reluctance to meet the inevitability of getting older and eventually dying, Alan's latest book sheds light on the life-enhancing opportunities that beckon the over 60s. I have not always learned either quickly or well but I do intend to live the coming years with gratitude and generosity and* Not Fade Away *has already helped in this. Alan's book has touched and informed me. It has also signposted places I intend to visit; places that have patiently awaited my focused attention for some time and will now have to wait no longer.*

Mac Macartney, Founder of Embercombe
and author of *Finding Earth, Finding Soul*

It never ceases to astonish me that as a child I was never taught how to grow old. Yet here I am approaching 60 and discovering it really is an exceptional place to be! Of course time becomes a precious commodity but it shouldn't mean we stop experiencing the wondrous things in life. For me it is a time of reconnection with my inner teenage rebellion as I fight off all the negative perceptions thrown at me from the media about ageing. Age is a privilege!

Age is a journey, as if we are fine tuning our inner spirit, becoming the culmination of the decades we have lived. It should be a celebratory experience. We live in an exceptional time, where technology and science enables the human body to live beyond its means through communication, allowing us all the ability to explore, even if we cannot physically travel for example. I don't think we fade away at all, if anything we should burn brighter with a life time of knowledge and a focus to enjoy and explore every moment. Alan's message comes from personal experience and as I am fast catching up, I cannot reiterate it more strongly...LIFE IS FOR LIVING.

Toyah Willcox, *singer and actress*

I feel lucky to have been part of the Sixties. I feel lucky to still be singing what Bob Marley calls "these songs of freedom". And in the autumn of my years I'm glad I can reach out and find a song to sing. Growing old is a challenge and Alan's book can make the journey less daunting and more fun.

I have been singing professionally for 54 years (since 1964). It has been said that when one is creative, one is closer to the creator. I believe this to be true, but it has only been in the last ten to fifteen years that I have come to understand this concept. When I am singing and playing guitar live for an audience there is a magic that happens. A kind of communion. Alan's book talks about the usefulness of prayer and for me, singing live is my way of praying. As Alan explains, the word 'prayer' can refer to the many different ways you can "connect to any power you feel is greater than you". I feel the world (at last) is moving toward the feminine and this opens the gates for both women and men to get in touch with their creative spirit.

Julie Felix, *singer and activist*

NOT FADE AWAY

Staying happy when you're over 64!

by ALAN HEEKS

THIS BOOK IS DEDICATED TO THE SPIRIT
OF THE 1960s: MAY ALL OF US FIND THE
LOVE, PEACE AND FREEDOM THAT OUR
GENERATION DREAMED OF THEN.

CONTENTS

Acknowledgements

I WANT TO THANK the landscapes and music, as well as the people, who have enabled me to write this book.

Hazel Hill is a 70-acre wood which I bought at the age of 39, when my business career suddenly produced some capital. For thirty years, this magical wood has guided and nourished me through many crises and discoveries. It has taught me to listen to the land, to commune with Nature, and I'm glad that it has helped so many others too.

Where I live in West Dorset, the intricate landscapes of valleys and hills, the golden cliffs and empty foreshores, all keep me steady and fresh. And my visits to Dentdale and the Settle and Carlisle railway always lift my spirits.

If you ask what I recall from the 1960s, the first thing is the music. Watching The Who, The Supremes, Small Faces, on *Top of the Pops*. The first time I heard Sergeant Pepper, wild nights with The Doors, Jefferson, Janis Joplin. This music has never left me, and it really has inspired this book, as you'll see from the chapter titles.

My own creative ageing journey has been hugely helped and brightened by friends, family and colleagues. I specially want to thank Marcos Frangos, Jane Sanders and Nayyer Hussain for both friendship and advice. My parents have been fine role models for ripening with age. My daughters, Ella and Fran, give me a lot of delight and insights. And my wife Linda supports me in more ways than I can name. Deep thanks to you all.

The support team who've helped produce this book have been great. Special thanks to Nikki Pepperell, my PA, to Bernard Chandler, designer and '60s veteran, to Will Gethin, Louise Mossman, Sarah Acton, and others on publicity. And to all of you for buying this book.

Special appreciation goes to the many people who have shared their life stories with me over the years, including those featured in Chapter 18, My Generation.

FOREWORD
by Mervyn Stutter

"If you can remember the Sixties then you weren't really there."

THAT'S WHAT PEOPLE SAY ISN'T IT? WELL, THEY'RE WRONG. If you can remember the Sixties it means you're still alive. And good for you!

It's a real pleasure to be asked to write a foreword to this book. The rich theme of 'ageing flower children' has always been part of my scriptwriting and songwriting both in my touring shows and my radio comedy series: *Love 40 – New Balls Please* (Radio 2) and *Getting Nowhere Fast* (Radio 4).

Alan's general theme in this book is creative ageing and as an entertainer I have been exploring the humour and poignancy in that for some years. (From the time I turned 40 actually. Long time ago now – don't ask). With the Beatles, the World Cup and the Moon Landings, we grew up believing anything and everything was possible. That's how we were in the Sixties, so why stop now!

OK so we're all getting old. No, correction, we're all getting older, much older than ever before. We're the Children of the Sixties in our seventies and the Children of the Seventies in our sixties and we could live to over 90, something our parents could rarely do. So there's no roadmap for us. We'll have to make it up as we go along. We invented teenage, we reinvented middle age and now we are reinventing old age and Alan's book is here to help.

In his chapter Love Me Do, Alan starts by placing us into handy vinyl sections depending on our current "status" – as we now say on Facebook. Long play, Re-release, Single singles and Seeking singles. I'm definitely Long Play now – 30 years and counting - but I've been all the others as well!

And any one of us could be again. There's more divorce in the Over 60s than ever before. But then again it does mean there's a lot more divorcees back in the Singles Section. Think positive! So tear off that old dust jacket, ignore the scratches, enjoy the crackles and get ready to play again - and don't ask this question as I did in one of my songs:

"Why do men and women want to live together
They just end up naked, talking about the weather
Or going to Relate or dressing up in leather
Why do men and women bother?"

We bother because falling in love is a wonderful thing and we all love to be loved.

"Men and women don't get along
Women are right men are wrong
That's it – end of song."

OK, so if that's the case, then maybe your Dansette is stuck on repeat and it's time to lift the needle and try another track. In his chapter Won't Get Fooled Again, Alan advises on how to 'change the story' – how to break those habits that are clearly not serving us well.

And it is worth it. Most marriages after 60 are very successful. After all, 'Till death us do part' may not be too big a commitment when you're 75. No, I'm not being glib, death is in the back of our thoughts for all of us these days. Never mind "I hope I die before I get old", we should be yelling "I hope I get old before I die."

I certainly do. So we all try to do the healthy things. (Check out Chapter 10 and see how you're doing.) We run marathons, swim with dolphins, climb Kilimanjaro or skydive and bungee. We meditate, do yoga, we Rumba and we Zumba, eat our 5 a day and relax with a glass of red wine. (Apparently it's very good for the heart. Phew! Cheers everybody!) But the rest of us are more likely to be found lolloping along a treadmill in an old Def Leppard T shirt and floral beach baggies watching Judge Rinder. And we do all this in the hope that we live longer, or even better that we stay healthy while we're living longer.

And if we don't, well, it seems that many of us are planning for that as well. The Children of the Sixties are now reinventing the funeral. And why not? We're choosing the words, the songs and the settings. We want it all to be a party, a celebration of our lives. We want to be carried in to Stayin' Alive and the curtains to close to Great Balls of Fire – at volume 11. We want our ashes fired into the sky in a rocket or dug into the ground to feed our favourite oak. Most of all, of course, we want to be remembered.

> *"I want people to cry at my funeral*
> *I want people all snotty with grief*
> *I want people to say 'God how I miss him'*
> *I want people to lie through their teeth*
> *I want lots of lovely obituaries*
> *Coz it's only when you're dead – that you sell more CDs"*

Bette Davies said "Old age ain't no place for sissies" but we Baby Boomers were reared on free school milk and orange juice and shedloads of optimism. We will be fearful and alone at times but we are creative and positive and that is the ethos of Alan's book.

> *"But why worry about old age, it doesn't last long"*

But these days it does and it will and we'll need all the help we can get. So here is Not Fade Away – the essential roadmap for all Post Menopausal Flower Children. Rock on people!

Mervyn Stutter

The song lyrics quoted in italics are from Mervyn Stutter's CDs.
For further information visit
www.mervynstutter.com

Chapter One

Rave On: finding your way in the vintage years

HOW DO YOU FEEL about your late sixties, or being in your seventies? It's a big transition: maybe a time of new freedom, but also a time for facing challenges. That's why finding *your* way at this age matters: you'll need to find the upsides for yourself!

If you were born in the 1940s or 1950s, you probably grew up with the Biblical idea that three score years and ten is the normal life span. Back then, many people did die in their sixties or seventies. So to be alive and moderately healthy at 70 is a surprise – it gives a sense of being on borrowed time, or going off the map.

The aim of this book is to offer you some simple, practical maps to find your bearings and make sense of the sixties and seventies. It's an age that brings some new worries for most of us, but also an age when we have more choices and resources than we may realise.

This book won't tell you what to think or how to be. It will offer you new skills, new ways to understand your situation, and draw on experience from others. I've been leading personal development workshops, and taking part in them, for twenty-five years, so I've shared deeply in many people's life stories, as well as exploring my own.

I'm writing this book for myself as much as anyone. My seventieth birthday is only months away, and I'm apprehensive. Despite being an optimist at heart, there's a lot about being this old that's bothering me. So this book is a true exploration for me too, and I hope it enables us all to be truly happy at 70 and beyond.

Using this book

This is a self-help book: it's intended to help you to live more happily, and work through issues which are bothering you. The book has three main sections. First, *Finding your Gifts*, to help you appreciate the benefits in your life, add to them, and use your resources. Secondly, *Digging the Challenges*, which offers you ways to understand and work on difficulties. Lastly, *Fresh Maps*, which provides some new tools for understanding, and includes insights and advice from a range of people.

My allocation of topics between gifts and challenges has to be a guess, and won't fit for everyone. In any case, some parts of your life, such as family, may be both a boon and a problem. I've tried to address both upsides and downsides for all topics.

There are many ways to use this book, including reading it right through, or diving into the topic that's of most interest. However, if you're reading this book to resolve a problem, I suggest spending some time looking at *Finding your Gifts* first. Appreciating positives about yourself and your life can give you better morale and confidence to dig into a challenge.

You'll find a number of self-help methods and checklists all through the book. It may be helpful to ask a friend to support you with some of these processes: a second perspective and help from someone else can make it easier. Keeping a journal of your insights and progress may also be useful.

Using this book: if you're not a Baby Boomer

Although this book is focussed on readers age 64 to 75, much of it should be helpful for readers younger or older than this. Here are some tips on using the book for other age groups.

Under 50: this book can help you understand and relate to parents, colleagues, friends who are from a quite different generation. You may just see the Baby Boomers as a privileged group who had State benefits you'll never see: that may be true, but there's a fuller picture which this book can show you. The other benefit could be a sense of what's ahead for you, which could help shape your priorities.

50-63: I see this as the midlife transition phase, which has some different issues from 64-75. However, some factors, like changing family dynamics, are similar. This age group may benefit a lot from appreciating the next life stage that's coming towards them.

75 plus: these days, there are many people in their seventies, eighties and beyond who are still healthy and active, and who will find a lot of this book relevant. While seventy may be a classic transition point, making the changes later is better than not at all!

Landscapes of life: the 70 watershed

One inspiration for this book was my 93-year-old mother telling me how she finds old age a good time for making sense of the landscapes of her life. Even at the younger stage of 70, this idea of looking back over your life like a series of landscapes feels helpful.

The term watershed is often used for a big transition: literally, it means a ridge or high point in a landscape, from which rivers flow in opposite directions. Can you find a physical landscape image for how turning 70 feels for you? My image is from a favourite drive west of Salisbury, where the A354 climbs and curves up a small valley, out of the lowlands, until the road runs high along the chalk downs with views for miles, across valleys, towards far hills.

What this image means for me is climbing out of complexity, and also leaving other people (the lowland villages) somewhat behind: emerging into a clear, wide space with few defining features, where I can see all round me: back to the past, ahead of me, and off to both sides.

This is not a landscape where many people live: it's beautiful, but bare and windswept up here. I believe that turning 70 offers us a chance to find this clear space, get more perspective, leave some baggage behind, and make some conscious choices about where we set our direction for the years ahead. This includes friendships, partnership, and our whole social network, which get more important at this age.

The various chapter topics should help you in this process. And keep in mind the idea of finding **your** way forward. One benefit of these uncertain times is that patterns and precedents are breaking down, so we're more free to suit ourselves. There are people starting families and big new projects in their seventies; there are people relishing a quieter, slower pace; and there are people facing death or major illness.

Whatever you're facing, believe that you have more choices, more resources, more support than you imagine. Trust that life is inviting you to find *your* way, whatever that may be.

Self-help process 1: Three wishes

Imagine there's an Ageing Fairy who pops out of this book, and offers you three wishes: whatever you want that would help you at this life stage. Just write down what comes up for you:

1. _____
    FIND PURPOSE — NEW DIRECTION
    _____
    _____

2. _____
    _____
    _____
    _____

3. _____
    _____
    _____
    _____

Use these three wishes to guide the way you use this book.
Believe that magic can happen, your wishes may come true.

RESOURCES

You'll find a guide to further resources at the end of most chapters. This is a short book, so it can't cover topics in depth, but it can show you ways to do that.

There are three books I recommend for a deeper overview:

▮ **The Warmth of the Heart Prevents Your Body from Rusting: Ageing Without Growing Old**
by Marie de Hennezel. ISBN-13: 978-190574484-8
One of the best books I've found on ageing: especially useful for the young-old, who, as Marie observes, are often terrified of being old-old. This is a positive, practical guide to enjoying life at any age beyond fifty.

▮ **New Passages: Mapping Your Life Across Time**
by Gail Sheehy. ISBN-13: 978-000255619-4
This is a brilliant overview of the sequence of life stages which most people go through, with the differences for men and women, and insights on how to face them more easily.

▮ **Out of the Woods: A Guide to Life for Men Beyond 50**
by Alan Heeks. ISBN-13: 978-184528512-8
Don't let the title deter you: a lot of this book is relevant for women and men in their sixties and seventies, and it covers many of the topics in *Not Fade Away* in a lot more depth.

Part 1

FINDING YOUR GIFTS

Chapter Two

Love Me Do:
reinventing partnership

Well she was just seventeen, you know what I mean,
And the way she looked was way beyond compare,
Well I couldn't dance with another, oooh, when I saw
her standing there.

I knew that he was mine, so I gave him all the love that I had.
And someday soon he'll take me home to meet his mom
and his dad.

LOVE CAN STILL BE WONDERFUL in our later years, but we have to let go of some baggage first – like all the simplistic ideals from the pop songs of our youth. We can't expect our partner to look like a twenty-something film star, and we're unlikely to find instant sexual fireworks (remember the song *Wild Thing*?).

The pop songs of the sixties gave us one ideal of love – a boy and a girl, together forever. Now, the possibilities are endless. In this chapter we'll explore four main ones:

Long play: a partnership which has lasted for much of your adult life, probably more than 30 years.

Re-release: people in a second or third long-term committed relationship.

Single singles: those who are not in a partnership, and are not looking for one.

Seeking singles: people wanting another relationship, possibly through online dating sites and blind dates.

Long-term partnerships: the art of the possible

My first marriage lasted a creditable 25 years, but I slightly envy the couples I've met who are still together after 30, 40 or even 50 years. There's no one answer to how to do this, so forgive some generalisations.

Unless both partners are emotionally dead, it's likely that sustaining a really long-term partnership will need a lot of tolerance and creativity. As one man in a 41-year marriage told me: "We've had to drop the big and small resentments that build up. If you can't focus on positives, and love each other as you are, you'll be living in an acid bath."

The level of tolerance you need can vary widely. It might mean living through a partner having an affair, or both of you having a six-month sabbatical. It might just mean accepting that you spend less time together, because your interests are diverging.

As a long-term couple move into their late sixties and beyond, finding a new shared interest seems important. You need to renew the togetherness alongside giving each other more space.

Re-release: the second (or third) time around

Divorce statistics show that the fifties and sixties are now peak ages for marriages to end, whereas twenty years ago the peak time was the forties. Many people in their later years are in a second or third, long-term committed relationship. This can add new positives and new complications.

Having one major relationship fail seems to give people a strong motivation to make it work next time. Understanding habits and patterns which caused the original breakup is crucial: we've probably all seen new couples unhappily repeating old stories. There are a lot of good books and therapists who can help you to avoid repeating history: see *Resources* on page 13.

The potential complications may include how each of you relate to your own ex and your partner's, and how to navigate the extended family around you. Hopefully as you get older, you can focus on the good history not the old pain, and on happiness in the present.

One benefit of being a newer long-term couple may be scope for more dialogue, more give-and-take, in how you want the relationship to be, now and in the future. This should preferably include how to handle things if one partner has major health problems. See more on this in *Chapter 10*.

Single singles: the happy one

I meet quite a few people in their late sixties or older who are happily single, and expect to stay that way. I believe the secret to this is understanding what kinds of connection you do want, and setting up your life to provide them. Here are some examples:

- A good circle of friends with shared interests
- Having a companion: a friend who's sometimes an intimate partner too
- Being part of a faith group or other network who give you whatever qualities of community you need

Seeking singles: silver dating?

I still recall how tough it was to find myself single at 50, plunging into soulmates ads and blind dates. Now, you'll find plenty of soulmates ads from people in their sixties and seventies. There's an extensive guide to mature dating and relationship skills in my book *Out of the Woods*.

My top tip is to get yourself to a position where a relationship is a nice-to-have, not an urgent necessity. Learn to look after yourself, build up your friendships, and see every date as an adventure not an ordeal. And don't pour out all your troubles on a first date!

Here's looking at you, kid

A big adjustment for any relationship at this age is about looks. Neither you nor your partner will look young: if you struggle to find attraction when you look at a face with lines and wrinkles, realise the other person is looking at your face too. If you can find the humour in this situation, you're doing well.

My advice is, focus on touch and emotion to deepen intimacy, more than looks. If you can both find real love and compassion, for yourself and the other, *as you are*, you won't mind the wrinkles.

Stuck in a groove?

As a couple get older, the scope for mismatch, letdown, resentment grows. Maybe one partner wants a busy social life, and the other now wants to stay quietly at home. Maybe one partner is fit and active, while the other is unwell and needs care.

You may feel that it's hard enough meeting your own needs, and now there are rising demands from your partner. It's easy to start sulking and complaining. Here are a few tips that may help:

- *Do what you can, and draw the line:* don't damage or exhaust yourself in meeting your partner's needs. You're entitled to say no, have a life of your own, ask others for help.
- *Dig for gratitude:* try hard to find even small positives you can appreciate about your partner and your life together.
- *Find a smile:* even grim situations can have a funny side, and laughter melts tension magically. Remember Victor Meldrew: notice if you're getting too serious, and send yourself up when necessary
- *Remember compassion:* treating your partner as you'd like to be treated can help you find the love and sympathy. It will nourish both of you far more than resentment.

Breakin' up is hard to do

Major separations rarely happen by complete mutual agreement. More often, one partner is pushing for it, and the other resisting. Sometimes one partner looks obviously to blame, by an affair, addictions and so on. Probably neither of you will have any precedent for this crisis, and your emotional and negotiating skills will be overwhelmed. Whatever part you're playing in the drama, find as much compassion as you can for both of you, and go many extra miles to maintain some goodwill in your separation.

One reason this is traumatic is that you're probably facing a deep emotional crisis at the same time as negotiating on a mass of financial, legal and other matters, ranging from who keeps the house to equally massive questions like how you share the DVD collection. You need good support on all fronts.

RESOURCES

I have tried over 100 writers about relationships, and Harville Hendrix is the best I've found. There's also a lot of useful inform-ation and tools on **www.harvilleandhelen.com** and **www.imagorelationships.org**

▌ **Getting the Love You Want: a Guide for Couples**
by Harville Hendrix. ISBN-13: 978-067171529-8
This will help you understand the basic dynamics of relationships, such as what attracts partners to each other. It has a good section on dealing with crises and a ten-step process for deepening intimacy, based on a series of excellent exercises which can be done over ten weeks.

▌ **Keeping the Love You Find: a Guide for Singles**
by Harville Hendrix. ISBN-13: 978-067173420-6
This is also excellent, with a set of well-grounded exercises to help you both understand and heal some of your wounds and negative patterns about relationships, and learn skills to start and sustain a more intimate relationship.

▌ **Men are from Mars, Women are from Venus**
by John Gray. ISBN-10: 072252840-x
I refused to read this for several years because the title sounded so corny. In fact, I found a lot of helpful wisdom for men and women, and ways to describe problems so that partners can talk about them.

▌ **Sexy Seniors – Sex after 60!**
by Lucinda Treves. ASIN: B00PJCR0HA
If you can get over the cringey title, this is a short, common-sense e-book covering basic issues.

▌ **DIY Sex & Relationship Therapy**
by Lori Boul. ISBN-13: 978-184528474-9
A delightfully clear, positive self-help book designed for couples to work through together. It has a cheerful, no-jargon approach and covers a range of key issues, including basic communication, handling conflicts, and a good long section on sexual issues, including healing processes.

▌ **Better Relationships: Practical Ways to Make Your Love Last**
by Sarah Litvinoff. ISBN-13: 978-009185670-0
Published by Relate, this is a good basic guide to relationship dynamics, including the challenges of long-term relationships.

▌ **The Good Divorce: Keeping Your Family Together When Your Marriage Falls Apart**
by Constance Ahrons. ISBN-10: 0747514712
A valuable guide to handling a breakup without permanent damage to the partners or the family. It's also good on how to cope if your partner is withdrawn or hostile.

▌ **Divorce and Splitting Up: A Complete Legal and Financial Guide**
by Claire Colbert. ISBN-13: 978-184490034-3
A thorough guide to the UK legal and financial practicalities, including sections on cohabiting couples, maintenance, differences in Scotland and Northern Ireland, and how to minimise legal costs by drafting agreements yourself.

Chapter Three

You've Got a Friend: pals in maturity

When you're down and troubled,
And you need some loving care,
And nothing, nothing is going right,
Close your eyes and think of me,
And soon I will be there
To brighten up even your darkest night.

DO **YOU PREFER** the Carole King original, or the hit version by her mate James Taylor? It still brings tears up for me, 46 years on. And I've always wondered, who is saying these wonderful words: is it just a friend, or a lover, or a guardian angel? Is it what we need to say to ourselves? In later life, we need all these four kinds of friend.

Friendships can be one of the big upsides of the vintage years: hopefully you've got time to relax and enjoy them. *Last of the Summer Wine* gives us one role model, with gentle adventures, and reminiscences. But at this age, friends may also matter because of the practical and emotional support you can give each other.

The need to cultivate your friendships makes even more sense now. I've seen surprisingly deep bust-ups, even between long-standing friends. As your sense of time feels shorter, and you're clearer what matters in life, you may become more choosy about friends, and may need to find some new ones.

Looking at patterns

Are you a giver, taker or receiver? Many people are stuck in one of these roles, but you need to balance all three. Givers (often martyrs) exhaust themselves looking out for others, secretly hoping they'll receive in return. Takers will grab, demand, fight for what they want: sometimes necessary, but often not. Receiving can be hard for some: letting in the things you need, trusting without control.

Give yourself a helicopter view of your patterns and habits with friends. Which of these three roles do you play? Can you see other habits: do you make new connections easily, or stick with a few long-term ones? Do you fall out with friends and groups, or lose interest quickly? Do you feel unheard, left on the margins? If you don't like what you see, set your intention to change it. Maybe you're repeating a negative story like rejection in your friendships and group roles. Perhaps you resist going deeper because you lack the social skills, or you fear you'll be rejected when you show the real you. Friendship can be as challenging as your main relationship, and actually needs some of the same skills.

Friends: Oiling the gearbox, topping the cake

One of the big improvements in my fifties and sixties has been more and better friendships. I feel very fortunate to have a few deep friendships, plus a lot of pretty good ones: most with men, but a few with women. These friendships oil the gearbox of life: lubricating changes, conflicts and crises which could otherwise be overwhelming. They also top the cake, through the pleasures of companionship, and by witnessing and appreciating good things about me which I often ignore. This may sound easy, but it hasn't been for me. I've had to learn by mistakes and the painful loss of some good friendships.

Looking back at my 30s and 40s, I see how awkward I was to be friends with: so uptight, over-sensitive, unsure of myself, self-centred, controlling... It has taken a lot of change, both deliberate and unplanned, to improve things: men's groups, co-counselling, divorce and lost friendships have all helped.

Like me, you may know people who seem naturally sociable, and always have plenty of friends. This section is not for them, but for anyone who needs to work at this, especially those who suffer from shyness, depression or other problems with self-confidence. Even small rebuffs can hurt like hell. Think of this like a child learning to walk: a few tumbles and bruises are only natural. And if you're struggling to find the motivation, remember that the skills you learn in friendship will help you in other arenas, like romance and work.

Here are my top tips on cultivating friendship:

❖ ***Be willing to experiment:*** trying a range of approaches with a variety of people increases your chances of success.

❖ ***Realise that there are many kinds of friendships:*** Be aware of the various kinds you would like, and try to sense early on what your potential friend wants. For example, the level of openness and emotional sharing may vary hugely. In many male friendships, all this is unspoken: remember *Last of the Summer Wine.*

❖ ***Imagine a new friendship as a spiral process:*** don't plunge in, but let it deepen gradually. Listen for clues from your friend about the subjects they do and don't want to talk about, and guide them on your preferences.

❖ ***Cultivate your listening skills:*** try to hear what your friend is saying, and respond to it. Don't get preoccupied with your own nerves and needs. Listen for what's not being said: many people struggle to express their feelings or ask for support, so listen for clues and make an offer, for example, "Would it help you to talk more about the divorce?".

❖ ***Co-counselling training*** can help with friendship skills, including negotiating contracts. This may sound formal, but it's simply about getting clear expectations between you. Checking what your friend would like from you shows that you care about their needs.

❖ ***Find the courage to make the first move:*** In shifting from casual contact towards friendship, someone needs to take the initiative: Remember the other person may be even more shy than you are.

❖ Sometimes, especially for men, doing something together can be an easier start to a friendship than sitting and talking. It could be quite simple, like going to a film, or having a walk.

❖ Remember the question early in this Chapter about the Giver, Taker and Receiver roles: do you and your friend have a balance between these? If you are stuck in one role, experiment with changing.

❖ As a friendship starts to build, if you want it to deepen, try talking openly with your friend about how it's going and what you both want from it. This kind of frankness doesn't come easy in our culture, but it can help both of you to get what you need, and to learn as you go along.

❖ As you change, the kind of friends you want will change too. If you want to move from friendship down to acquaintance, do it honestly: talk it through with your friend, hear their feelings, try to reach a point of completion and celebration for the friendship. This will cause less pain than just stopping.

I hear you knocking: communication skills

You may feel you're late in life to learn new skills and change your ways, but improving your communication skills will help a lot in friendships, partnerships, and other aspects of your life and work. What this means is expressing strong feelings and difficult views so that others can hear and consider them, listening to others so you really hear them and they know it, and handling conflicts constructively. See more in *Resources* opposite.

* * *

RESOURCES

▌ Co-counselling

You start by taking a Fundamentals training in basic methods of communication, e.g. expressing emotions, hearing them and clearing them. In co-counselling, you and another person take turns to counsel each other, with equal time for each person, but the skills are useful in all kinds of situations. See **www.co-counselling.info**
The website explains what co-counselling is, what the training involves and offers excellent download material.

▌ How to be Assertive in Any Situation

by Sue Hadfield and Gill Hasson. ISBN-13: 978-027373849-7
One of the most highly rated books on the topic. It provides a good grounding in communication and assertiveness skills for relationships and other situations.

▌ How to Win Friends and Influence People

by Dale Carnegie. ISBN-13: 978-009190681-8
This book was first published in 1936! Its style may seem antique, but there's sound advice on making friends.

Chapter Four

Get It Together: finding your communities

WHAT DOES COMMUNITY MEAN TO YOU? It's an over-used word, but as we get older, it becomes more vital. I see the essence of community as mutual support: helping each other, sharing resources, gathering collective wisdom. You may find these qualities in the local community where you live, in shared interest groups like a gardening or sports club, shared values groups like a church or meditation group, or in a work organisation, and in your family and friends.

Why does community matter so much in these times? Because everything's getting more uncertain, and the safety net of services is being badly eroded by funding cuts. Health, social services, environment – you name it. Before the Welfare State, communities did these things, and now they need to again.

And why does community matter more as we get older? Firstly, because our need for help increases. Secondly, because we may have more time to give to our communities. Thirdly, because we have to seek out community more actively and consciously in later years: in middle age, work and kids often bring us connections easily.

It's worth asking yourself, why might community be important for me now? How could it enrich my life, meet my needs, help me share my talents? To get you started, here are some of the potential benefits community can offer:

* * *

■ *Practical support:* if you break a leg, you'll need help with shopping, transport or more. This is part of the give and take of many communities.

■ *Emotional support:* when we're stressed or upset, it helps a lot if someone can listen, sympathise, and give us perspective. With ageing, that support matters even more.

■ *Collective strength:* if your neighbourhood gets flooded, or is threatened by service cuts, you need a group of people to pull together, and look out for the common good.

■ *Fellowship:* there's a simple pleasure in companions, shared interests and values.

■ *Insights:* when a situation baffles you, the wisdom of a group of people, especially elders, often can see a way through it.

Seven kinds of community

The word community has so many meanings. Put simply, a community is any group of people, informal or formal, who have some shared interests, aims or values. Here are seven kinds of community, to help you recognise the ones you're part of:

1 *Family and Friends:* if you look at the benefits of community listed above, you'll hopefully feel you get some of these from family and friends.

2 *Local Neighbourhood:* some local neighbourhoods are close-knit communities, others hardly at all. I recall a friend who lived for several years in a street in North London where no one spoke to each other. She rented a hall and invited everyone to a party: over half the residents came, and suddenly it became a community who looked out for each other, loaned stuff, enjoyed each other's company.

These days, it's hard to foresee what problems or blessings might affect your neighbourhood, but you'll all be more resilient if you have some sense of community.

And if your locality doesn't feel like a community, believe it could change.

3 **Shared interests:** this might include sports clubs, gardening, yoga. Such groups are a kind of community, because you have regular social contact, a sense of fellowship, and some scope for mutual support. U3A (University of the Third Age) is an example of a network of many shared interests, for older people.

4 **Shared values:** this may overlap with shared interests, but a group with shared values is likely to have deeper trust and insights, and more willingness to help each other in hard times. Examples of shared values would be a sustainability group like Transition Towns, a Buddhist meditation group, or a cancer support group. Seeing these as a community, not just a group, can help you understand how it works, and how people can get the best from it.

5 **Work organisations:** I've spent many years involved in work teams, as a manager and a trainer. Many work teams don't have community qualities, but some of the best teams do.

6 **Vision community:** this means a group of people drawn together by a shared vision which they want to sustain or bring to fruition. In the pioneering projects I've created, the vision community has been vital in providing the momentum and insights to achieve the dream. So if you have a big goal, or are supporting someone else with one, the vision community can really help it happen.

7 **Intentional community:** this term is used to describe communities with a formal organisation structure, which require people to commit to a code of values, and where people are living together. Intentional communities may be loose-knit, like an eco-village, or intense, like a commune or a monastery. They're a very useful source of wisdom for informal communities of all kinds.

Taking an overall view of how communities and groups fit in your life may be something new but it's worth exploring, both to meet your needs and to make a contribution.

The fellowship of elders

Getting older can be lonely and bewildering sometimes. The mutual support and wisdom of groups can help hugely with this. Here are some ways to find this kind of community:

- Just invite a few people of your age to join you for tea: explain that you'd like to talk together about ageing. It might turn into a regular group!
- Look for a men's or women's group where most members are over 50: an ongoing group like this can offer a lot of experience and support.
- Try a workshop on creative ageing, like the ones I run at Hazel Hill Wood and Findhorn.
- Find a local shared interest or support group relevant to your situation.

RESOURCES

COMMUNICATION SKILLS AND GROUP DYNAMICS
▌ **The Red Book of Groups**
by Gaie Huston. ISBN-13: 978-095103233-6
This is an outstandingly short, simple book which covers a lot
of essential points.

LEARNING FROM INTENTIONAL COMMUNITIES
▌ **Creating a life together**
by Diana Leafe Christian. ISBN-13: 978-086571471-7
This book grows from decades of experience and dozens of
communities. Whilst it's a how-to guide for starting an
intentional community, the sections on community principles
and dynamics are invaluable for all kinds of community, and
the best book I know on the subject.

▌ **www.diggersanddreamers.org.uk**
If you want to learn more about intentional community, and
visit some, this website is the best directory of UK projects,
related books and more.

FINDING CONTACTS NEAR YOU
▌ **Action for Happiness** have many local groups around the
UK: a great way to find a congenial community of people
near you: see **www.actionforhappiness.org**

▌ **Age UK** have listings of local Friendship Centres and forums
for practical information: see **www.ageuk.org.uk**

▌ **University of the Third Age** has local groups and a huge
variety of courses across the UK: see **www.u3a.org.uk**

Chapter Five

WE ARE FAMILY: WHO ARE YOU NOW?

HOW WOULD YOU PICTURE YOUR FAMILY? Some people see a sitcom or a movie. I see a cross between an octopus and an amoeba: complex, always subtly moving, hard to define. Families can change suddenly or slowly: in your vintage years, you may be responding to change more often than you create it. Every family has its own shape or flavour. I can only offer insights on typical issues, so bear with me if they don't quite fit your situation.

You may feel squeezed between the needs of your ageing parents and your adult children. However, potentially your family can be a great source of love and support for everyone – including you. If that sounds far-fetched, use the sections below to help you face the issues in your family. Believe in the best, and believe that you can have some positive influence, at least!

Adult children

If you have children, and you're 65 to 75, your kids may well be in their twenties, thirties or forties. These are tough times for such age groups to create a stable home and income. You may find you're expected to keep providing support even when you need some yourself.

Your relationship with your children may have all kinds of flavours during your maturing years. They may resent you for growing up in easier times and being better off than they are. They may still expect you to make things right and bail them out.

Or you may find that the friendship between you deepens and that you help each other. This can be quite an edgy time between you and your kids, and it's a period when your relationship with them probably needs to be reinvented several times over.

Be honest about what's going on for you in your life generally, and if something feels awkward between you and your kids, name it and try to discuss it with them openly. Treat them more like adults: accepting that you and they have your own views and your own needs, and some balance needs to be found between them. You don't have to do everything for them and sacrifice yourself, but nor can you expect that they'll be completely independent of you. Here are some of the typical issues you may face.

- ✦ *Money.* Many people over sixty will be in a better financial position than their kids, although the kids' future earning potential is better than yours. Your kids may ask you to fund the deposit on a house or help pay off loans. You have to judge what's fair and if you want to set terms for any money you provide: it doesn't have to be a gift – you could make it a loan.
- ✦ *Fairness.* Do you remember when your kids were young how important it was to be fair and even-handed in what you gave them? For many kids, this remains a highly emotive issue, even when they're grown-up. You have to see these things from their viewpoint. The fact that one of your adult children has less money than another may not justify different treatment in their eyes.
- ✦ *Housing.* It may be great to have an adult kid still living with you, but for how long and on what terms? Is it fair to charge them rent? You may find yourself in edgy country, where you and your offspring have different views about what's a fair arrangement.
- ✦ *Crises.* It's only natural that the crises of your adult kids will affect you and probably involve you. They may have trouble finding a job or a career. It may be more serious:

depression, drugs and other ways of going off the rails. Your own feelings about the crisis may be aggravated by a sense that you've helped cause it, through the way you brought your kids up. However, it won't help your kids to face their problems if you take responsibility for them. Set your own feelings about the past aside, focus on supporting your son or daughter right now and help them take responsibility for their situation.

✚ ***Dates, partners, spouses – theirs.*** You may feel a loss as your kids find their main relationship outside the original family: try to embrace the new shape of things. The classic stress point is when you find your son or daughter's partner difficult or feel they are unsuitable. This is one case where honesty probably won't help. You'll fare better if you can support and accept them both as fully as you can.

✚ ***Dates, partners, spouses – yours.*** If you're no longer with the other parent of your children, connecting the kids with your new partner(s) is often tricky. It's only human to want your kids to approve of your new partner, and pretty natural for them to be guarded. Be patient. Over time, if they see you're really happy in this relationship, they're likely to open up to it.

✚ ***Grandchildren.*** Dynamics in the whole family change when your children have children, and mostly for the better. Parents often find that their relationship with their son or daughter becomes more adult to adult, more easy. Part of the change is that your own kids are now creating a family with its own values and culture. These may differ from the family you created. You might need to be careful to avoid passing on your own values and beliefs too strongly to your grandchildren.

* * *

Parents – ageing or dying

If you're age 65 to 75, you're probably supporting elderly, fragile parents or adjusting to their passing. One reason this can be hard is the reminders of our own ageing and dying in the years ahead.

At some stage as your parents age, it will help you all if you can start talking honestly about issues like care, dying, funerals and wills, as well as feelings. This kind of honesty is rare in British families, and your parents may be too upset and even embarrassed by their situation to initiate it. If such openness is unusual in your family, move towards it gently, choosing a minor issue to start with, accepting that you may be met with anger or silence at first.

Part of this honest conversation may be about care provision, before the need arises, and preferences about medical care, and whether they want to be resuscitated. Ideally, ask them to set up Lasting Powers of Attorney which mean that a family member or a friend can represent their views if they can no longer do so, and also can deal with financial and legal matters if they become incapacitated. See more on this in *Resources* on page 33.

In some ways you can prepare yourself for a parent's death, and in some ways it can't be anticipated. In the years before my father died, I talked to several friends about their feelings after a parent's death: it helped me understand how I might feel, and made me realise the qualities I wanted in my relationship with my dad before he went.

Other ways you can prepare are to say the things you need to, and talk openly about the practicalities: not only the will, but also about what kind of funeral, and who should be invited to the funeral. It can be helpful for you and your parent to discuss how they feel about dying and what they believe happens after death. In grieving my father, it uplifted me to know that he was calm about dying and positive about what lay beyond.

When a parent dies, brace yourself for a couple of extraordinary weeks. If you can make some space for your own grief, then do: but you're likely to find your time fully taken up with practicalities and other people. The funeral has to be organised. A lot of time goes in relatives and friends simply wanting to talk to you, share their feelings and be heard.

My advice about bereavement is that it's best to make time *after* the funeral to open up to your own feelings and then consider how your life moves forward from here. Take a few days off and rest. The passing of a parent is a life-changing experience, but nobody can foretell in what way for you. It may confront you with your own mortality and the sense that your generation is now the next to go, so this might be a call to face your own feelings about dying.

I found that the feelings of loss, sadness and confusion after my father died came back in waves: I made time to go into the emotions whenever I could. Marking the anniversary of a parent's death can be a good way of reconnecting with them, seeing what their life means to you now, and celebrating them, hopefully with other members of your family.

Brothers and sisters

Tensions with adult brothers and sisters are commonplace, but rarely discussed. These problems are usually long-standing, embarrassing and feel insoluble. Conflicts, roles and attitudes formed between children as they grow up in the original family can continue far into adult life.

Think about your own family. Did the oldest sister boss the other kids around? Did the youngest son have it easy and escape his share of duties? Can you see the same patterns decades later and are they still resented? As Jane Mersky Leder, author of a book on this subject says, 'Our siblings push buttons that cast us in roles we felt sure we had let go of long ago: the baby, the peacekeeper, the caretaker, the avoider... It doesn't seem to matter how much time has elapsed or how far we've travelled.'

The solution which many families adopt is that siblings (i.e. brothers and sisters) keep their distance from each other, and relate with superficial politeness. This is why Christmas, weddings and funerals can be the scene of family upsets. When you have large numbers of the family together for an extended time, with alcohol loosening the restraints, buried tensions erupt. If you're a witness to such upsets, remember that the two mature adults in front of you are really only a few years old.

Consider the roles and attitudes which you and your siblings took on in your childhood and teenage years. It's easier to blame the others, but recognise how your current behaviour and beliefs may continue the patterns. You alone cannot sweep away these habits, but if you change, it creates the possibility for others. Here are some hints on how to start the change:

◆ If you name the roles you still play and negative feelings you still carry towards your siblings, it creates a climate of honesty and a space where they can choose to do likewise. But don't expect an immediate matching response.

◆ When you and your siblings need to make a decision together, for example about care for your parents or selling the family home, suggest that you do it by consensus, treating everyone as equals. This can bring a more adult approach into the relations between you.

◆ When one of you needs to take a lead, suggest it should be the one with the most relevant skills and experience. Share tasks among you, for example in sorting out the estate after a parent has died. Again, this breaks old habits about who among the children should be responsible.

◆ Realise that you can influence your family dynamics, a bit. If your siblings are overemotional and always arguing, stay calm and adult. If they're always tight-lipped, let your own feelings show.

◆ If you have children of your own, look at the dynamics of your new family and compare them with your original one. Have some of the roles and attitudes passed down a generation? If so, do what you can to name them and clear this up with your children.

RESOURCES

▌ **You and Your Ageing Parents: How to Balance Your Needs and Theirs**
by Claire Gillman. ISBN-13: 978-034086424-1
A clear and thoughtful book which considers both emotional and practical issues, for ageing parents and for their children.

▌ **The Mental Capacity Act** gives all adults the right to decide for themselves about types of medical treatment: these preferences can be expressed in a Lasting Powers of Attorney and an Advance Decision. The best advice I've found on these complex topics comes from a charity, *Compassion in Dying*. The helpline is 0800 999 2434. They provide helpful publications, telephone help, and a useful website: **www.compassionindying.org.uk.**

▌ **What to Do When Someone Dies**
by Anne Wadey. ISBN-13: 978-184490127-2
This book gives a thorough explanation of how to register a death, who needs to be notified, how to organise the funeral, as well as probate and financial matters.

▌ **When Parents Die**
by Rebecca Abrams. ISBN-13: 978-072253131-0
A good book for handling the emotional impact of losing a parent.

▌ **Walking on Eggshells: Navigating the Delicate Relationship Between Adult Children and Parents**
by Jane Isay. ISBN-13: 978-076792085-8
A thoughtful, readable book about negotiating the balance between your own needs and your adult children. Also, a useful American website for many family issues, including parenting adult children, is: **www.troubledwith.com**

▌ Why Can't We Get Along? Healing Adult Sibling Relationships

by Peter Goldenthal. ISBN-13: 978-047138842-5

This gently explains the kinds of issues that arise among brothers and sisters in childhood, and offers strategies to try to heal them in later adult life. Also has a useful section for spouses, partners and other innocent bystanders of such conflicts.

Chapter Six

As Time Goes By: reaping the gifts of time

FOR MANY PEOPLE, the sixties and seventies bring more choice in how they spend their time. Retirement may feature in your work plans, and we'll explore its pros and cons below. Either way, you're hopefully at an age where pensions provide some income, and so you have less need to earn money.

On the other hand, there are people who find this life stage too busy. Elderly parents may need support. Your own health or your partner's may demand attention. Or you may find yourself pulled on by commitments to good causes or helping in your local community.

The aim of this chapter is to help you understand where your time is going, to learn to enjoy more free time, and make good choices about how you use your time. Having more time on your hands can be stressful, so we'll explore ways to enjoy slowing down, and how to spot a habit of filling your days with busyness. It's curious that we talk about *spending* time, which implies it would be dreadful to waste it: so we'll look at any *shoulds* that limit our choices.

If you currently feel overloaded with demands on your time, you may do best to start with the chapters on the issues creating the demands, before you read this one. This should help you reduce the time pressures. For example, try *Chapter 2* for relationship demands, *Ch.5* on family, *Ch.14* on work and money.

* * *

Self-help process 2: Time check

Answer the following questions with a score from:
-5 (not at all) to 5 (very much):   **Score**

a. Do you feel you have any free time, where you
    can choose what you do?

b. Are you happy overall about the way you use time?

c. Do you ever review and plan how you
    spend your time?

d. Is it easy for you to say no to requests for your
    time from other people?

e. Overall, how much do you feel you are choosing
    the ways you spend your time?

Total Score

Total up your score for all five questions: if it's a plus overall, you're already handling time well. If it's zero or less, there should be scope for progress.

Time has come today

Let's take a few minutes to consider what time is, and how there are different ways of experiencing time. This may seem an odd idea: in our society, linear time is such a dominant concept that you may not realise there are alternatives.

Linear time is the idea that one event follows another in a sequence, in chronological order: *first this happened, then that, then the other.* One pitfall of linear time is the illusion that each event is mainly *caused* by the one before it. Often, this is a poignant example of our human desire to force complex reality into a simple cause-effect story.

One of the gifts of older age I've seen in many people is a different sense of time, a kind of perspective and shape which is different from linear time. We might call this **parallel time**: it's a sense that all time periods – past, present, future, are in some way present and accessible to us at every moment in time, if we want this. This was beautifully expressed by T. S. Eliot:

"As we grow older
The world becomes stranger, the pattern more complicated
Of dead and living. Not the intense moment
Isolated, with no before and after,
But a lifetime burning in every moment."

Parallel time is a better way to understand our life than linear time. For example, when I start a new friendship now, my hopes and fears for it are coloured by many past friendships, from childhood onwards, and by my ideas of how this friendship may evolve in the future.

I was talking recently with my mother about the upsides of old age: she said that for her, one benefit is looking back across her life, and seeing how the different landscapes of it join up and fit together. This making-sense needs the quieter, more spacious time which we're more likely to find in later years.

A third idea is **cycle time**. Days, weeks and years all repeat in cycles which affect us. You may also find there are other cycles in your life: perhaps your friendships, jobs, hobbies come and go with a repeating cycle of time.

Slow time – quality time

You may know about slow food: it's a reaction against fast food, preferring fresh, natural, local cuisine, eaten and enjoyed *s l o w l y*. In later years, it's good to enjoy time slowly too: this can help you relax, and turn too much leisure into something positive.

A basic element of the slow time approach is to *experience each moment fully*, with all your senses. Give yourself space to enjoy every visual detail, each sound and smell, and any sensations of touch and taste. This is a form of the mindfulness meditations which are so popular now: being physically here and now is a great way to reduce the power of anxious thoughts which seem to be your whole reality.

Here are a few ideas for enjoying slow time:

- Cook yourself a special meal.
- Go for a slower, longer walk than usual.
- Let yourself relax with a bath or a massage.
- Write a letter, by hand!
- Try spending an hour or two aimlessly, lounging about.
- Next time you meet someone by chance, be willing to linger for a chat, especially if you rarely do so.

If these ideas seem crazy to you, because your time is crammed full of commitments, I suggest you review these demands carefully. Some people keep hectic because they're scared of being bored or unwanted. Even if you have major time priorities like caring for a parent or grandchild, remember that you have needs too, and you have a right to some time for them. At least aim for a few hours each week of time for you.

Is Should good?

A friend of mine recently retired at 67 from a demanding job in family social work. A few months later he told me he was worried, because he should be spending time doing something of service. Are there any *shoulds* in your attitudes to time? Try to recognise them and question their worth.

Often the shoulds are very old programming: recover your freedom of choice. Be realistic about all the time you've given to service, to work, to obligations, and claim your right to free time, slow time, fun time – at least for some of the time!

Chapter Seven

Running on Faith: gifts of inspiration

HAVE YOU EVER HAD TIMES when life felt pointless? Pretty dismal, isn't it? As we get older, we need to find a different kind of vision or purpose, about being, not doing. You may be pretty busy, you may have plenty of active years ahead of you, but... you know that's all going to end sometime. The people who impress me as elders have a presence, a still centre, an inner peace. These qualities seem to be their purpose, not achieving worldly fame or success.

In this chapter, I'll offer you some ways to see how inspiration can help you. This will include exploring a spiritual path: you may dislike the mere idea, but research shows that people who have some kind of faith or spiritual practice are typically more happy and resilient than those who don't.

Finding new vision: how Nature can help you

It's said that in sleep, sex and fishing, the more you try, the less happens. I've seen the same when I'm looking for a vision or a new sense of purpose. You can name what you want, but you can't make it happen.

What you *can* do is get yourself in a situation where you're relaxed, receptive, and the insight can come to you. This is where Nature can help. There's a lot of research that confirms the wellbeing benefits it provides, and there are specific ways to draw on Nature when you're seeking insights, for example:

Most Days.

✤ Spend at least one hour twice a week walking in nature, and better still, half an hour sitting still and silent (which some would call meditating).

✤ If there's an important question in your life that you're perplexed by, stop analysing and fretting about it, take a walk in nature, simply carrying the question, and being open to whatever insights you receive.

✤ Ask a tree! There are many people beside me who believe trees carry special wisdom and healing, which you can access if you are open and patient.

✤ For bigger questions around life purpose, or coming to terms with your own mortality, spend an extended time in Nature, just opening to insights: this is sometimes called a vision quest.

Role models for elderhood

Many of us have some negative feelings about ageing: we often ignore or deny it until we're forced to face it. Instead, look for positive role models: people who are positive and at ease with ageing, and even with its challenges.

Since I turned 60, I've deliberately looked for a few role models, ranging from a couple of years older than me, to six or eight years older, to fifteen years beyond me. I've nourished my friendship with them, and asked openly what I could learn from their experience. You can see some of their insights shared in *Chapter 18.*

Elderhood is a useful term for the qualities I admire in these friends, so let me explain what I mean by this. In traditional tribal cultures, men beyond warrior age and women beyond childbearing age were known as the elders. Whilst we often imagine tribes as hierarchies with a chief, many were guided by the elders as a group. Their role was to carry the history of the tribe, dream its dreams, talk with the spirit world, guide the young, speak the truth bravely.

This may look miles away from modern society but wouldn't both the young and old benefit if the over-60s were elders? What kind of personal qualities do elders have? Here are some that have touched me:

Presence	Self-respect	Patience
Listening	Maturity	Sweetness
Kindness	Light-heartedness	Courage

Connection to past, present and whatever's beyond death

The topic of elderhood is explored more fully in *Chapter 16*.

Spiritual paths: worth a try

For some older people, their spiritual path is a vital inspiration, a way of keeping centred, a big resource in facing problems. For others, the very idea is threatening or meaningless. I'm in the first of these groups, and I have friends in both of them. You should make your own choices, but if you don't have a spiritual path, it's worth exploring the possibility, and seeing if it could help you.

The term spiritual path means a set of beliefs and values, typically in some power or presence which is not material or measurable, which is bigger than individuals. One of the ways my spiritual path helps me is when I am upset or overwhelmed. Instead of being completely identified with the hurting part of me, which is usually the inner child, I can find my connection with my higher self: the divine spark in me which connects to the divinity in all life.

Another way a spiritual path helps is in finding direction and purpose. I believe we each have a soul that chooses the life we come into, including its blessings and problems. One of my prayers is to be guided so that my soul can serve the highest good of all, and align with divine purpose. If I feel lost, or in a problem situation, looking for the higher purpose in it can help.

In his excellent book, *The Power of Modern Spirituality*, William Bloom poses three questions which can help you recognise the spiritual aspects already in your life:

- *In what kind of circumstances do you most easily connect with the wonder and energy of nature and all existence, and feel your heart touched and your consciousness awakened?*
- *When is it easiest for you to retreat from activity, pause and reflect on your life, so as to manage your life and next steps?*
- *What are your highest values and how do you express them as a form of service for the community of life?*

He suggests three behaviours at the heart of all spiritual paths, whether or not these fit within a named tradition:

- *Connection* – sometimes, surely, your heart is touched and you connect with the wonder and energy of life.
- *Reflection* – sometimes already, you pause and reflect on your life and actions, and ponder how to change and improve.
- *Service* – and sometimes, of course, you have a clear sense of what is right and what is wrong, and you act so as to do good for others.

I've included William Bloom's ideas to show that you may already have a spiritual path, without calling it that. If so, you may find it helpful to develop it further. If not, exploring the possibility can be a fine adventure in itself.

In seeking a spiritual path you can meet some extraordinary people, make new friends, and learn a lot. Try out some different paths before you make a choice. Start by asking people around you: they may not talk about their beliefs until you ask them. Go to a few services, social events, or retreats. Read a few books. You'll find more pointers in Resources. If you are wary of being told what to do, explore paths like Buddhism, Sufism, Quakers and Unitarians.

Choosing a spiritual path is more a matter of letting it choose you. Try to get your logical mind and your ego out of the way, open up to a sense of where you're drawn to, what inspires you, and someone you can learn from. You may find the whole idea is not for you, but you may find a major source of wisdom and steadiness.

Spiritual gems: four for the road

One benefit of a spiritual path can be the wisdom of great teachers. Here are four gems, from different faiths, which have helped me:

Christian

You need to go back to Aramaic, the language Jesus spoke, to know the real depth of his teachings. Here's an expanded translation of lines 2 and 3 of the Lord's Prayer:

> **Netqadash shmakh.**
> *Help us breathe one holy breath feeling only you –*
> *this creates a shrine inside, in wholeness.*
> **Teytey malkutah.**
> *Create your reign of unity now – through our fiery hearts*
> *and willing hands.*

Sufi

Sufism is hard to sum up, as it's very inclusive, and has no one teacher or text. A central belief for many Sufis is the Arabic phrase: **La illaha ill'Allah**, which could be translated *There is nothing except divine unity.* It expresses a belief that divinity is beyond our human comprehension, and yet divine unity is in all life, at every moment.

Buddhist

There are many beautiful Buddhist mantras. One of my favourites is:

> **Om namo Amitabya**
> **Buddha ya, Dharma ya, Sangha ya**

This firstly involves the Amitabha Buddha as an embodiment or role model of the quality of compassion. Then it honours three major elements in many faiths: the teacher, the teachings, and the community of people who follow them.

* * *

Islamic

Few people realise how many beliefs are similar in Christian, Islamic and Jewish faiths, like the words for divine unity: *Alaha, Allah, Elohim.* This is my favourite line from the Fateha, the Moslem equivalent of the Lord's Prayer:

> **Ihdina sirat almustaqim.**
> *We ask you to reveal our next harmonious steps. Show us the path that says, "Stand up, get going, do it!". That resurrects us from the slumber of the drugged and leads to the consummation of Heart's desire, like all the stars and galaxies in tune, in time, straight on.*

This translation and the one for the Lord's Prayer are from the brilliant work of Neil Douglas-Klotz. See more in *Resources*.

Many people find it's helpful to connect with a great teacher, a wise soul, such as Jesus, Mother Theresa, Buddha, as a role model, an inspiration, someone to pray to. The teachings have their own insights and vitality alongside this. And a faith community can be a huge support, especially valuable as we get older.

How prayer can help

I'm using the word prayer very widely: to mean a way you could connect to any power you feel is greater than you. In these uncertain times, few of us think we're in control or all-powerful. If you have the humility to believe there's some greater power around us, why not pray to him, her or it? This can take many forms:

- 🌱 It's healthy to give prayers of thanks: especially when your previous prayers have been answered.
- 🌱 Try praying for others – not only people you know who need help, but for people and places in distress across the world. Your prayers may not solve the problem, but there's plenty of evidence that people feel supported by them.

❦ Pray for your needs, but be sensible! Ask for qualities, for guidance, for insights. *"Oh Lord, won't you buy me a Mercedes Benz"* was meant to be ironic!

❦ Sometimes it's better to offer a situation up, not pray for a specific outcome. For example: suppose your daughter's marriage is in crisis. Instead of you trying to decide the best outcome and praying for it, just pray that the crisis is resolved so that it serves the highest good of all involved.

RESOURCES

BOOKS

▌ **The Power of Now: A guide to spiritual enlightenment**
by Eckhart Tolle. ISBN-13: 978-034073350-9
One of the best-selling recent books in this field, and deservedly.

▌ **The Power of Modern Spirituality: How to live a life of compassion and personal fulfilment**
by William Bloom. ISBN-13: 978-074995285-3
A good guide to exploring and evolving your own spiritual path, and not linked to any one path or doctrine, with good resources for further exploration.

▌ **Prayers of the Cosmos**
by Neil Douglas-Klotz. ISBN-13: 978-006061995-4
This short and accessible book provides extended translations from Aramaic, the language Jesus spoke, which throw a different light on the essential teachings.

▌ **Desert Wisdom: A Nomad's Guide to Life's Big Questions from the Heart of the Native Middle East**
by Neil Douglas-Klotz. ISBN-13: 978-145651647-5
This brilliant book can help you understand and experience some of the deepest teachings from the spiritual traditions of the Middle East, including Sufi, Christian, Islamic, Jewish and others. It has helped my spiritual path for many years.

WEBSITES

Spiritual paths is a topic where web searches are likely to leave you boggled: focussing helps, e.g. results for Celtic spirituality are less confusing than spirituality in general.

▌ **www.abwoon.org** The website of Neil Douglas-Klotz, mentioned above.

▌ There are many different Buddhist orders active in the UK. Here are websites for a couple of them:
www.forestsangha.org
www.thebuddhistcentre.com
www.fpmt.org

▌ **Alternatives** at St James's Church in London offers a wide variety of evening sessions and longer workshops which can help you experience and explore different paths and teachers. See more at **www.alternatives.org.uk**

Chapter Eight

Born To Be Wild: fresh adventures

EVERYDAY LIFE these days can be uncertain and unsettling for anyone, and getting older may just seem to make that worse. It may feel tempting to settle into your rut, retreat into safety. In fact, you're likely to be more happy and resilient if you open up to fresh adventures.

I don't mean the kind of teenage lads' adventure where you nearly kill yourself. This is about trying something fresh, being someone new, having the courage to explore the unknown, both in yourself and around you. It's by exploring the new, even if it feels a bit risky, that you'll find fresh talents in yourself, make new friends, discover more insights.

Bucket lists seem popular these days: forty things to do before you die. They often include exotic physical adventures like sky-diving in Patagonia. I don't advocate this kind of jaunt: it's a lot of money, a massive carbon footprint, and is it really helping you grow?

There are three types of adventure explored in this chapter: *inner*, *outer*, and *social*. How can you tell what kind of adventures suit you? Here are a couple of ways you can check them:

? Do you have a sense of who you'd like to become, how you'd like to develop in the next few years?

? Is there a long-standing hope or dream from your youth that you might fulfil now?

? Do you have an interest or talent that you've never used, which you might develop at last?

 ? Can you identify an activity, person or place that you're a bit nervous about, but might be a fruitful adventure for you?

Adventures can have all kinds of aims. They can be about clearing old fears, resolving a conflict, or putting you in touch with a whole new side of yourself. Many of the chapters in *Part 2* and *Part 3* of this book could show you the opening to your next adventure.

Inner Adventures

I'm using this term to mean ways you can explore new aspects of yourself, discover new strengths, and work on parts of yourself that you find difficult. These kind of adventures won't cost money, and you can do them almost anywhere.

If you were preparing for a physical adventure, like a mountain trek, you'd prepare: you'd get the right maps and gear, you'd get fit, you'd have a plan of how to get to your destination, and back again. All of this has parallels for inner adventures: they need planning, provisions, and fitness too.

For inner adventures, this means starting with small, easy goals, and then building up. Here are a few examples to show you what an inner adventure might look like:

✔ Try some music, books, or a movie, that's unlike any you've tried before. Maybe pick a category at random, like steampunk…

✔ If you don't do meditation, try it – mindfulness and some other methods are designed for first-timers.
(*Chapter 7* may help with this).

✔ Experiment with slowing right down, and observing: watch the wind in the trees, or your own breath coming and going. See how much you can notice.

✔ Try observing yourself, kindly: try a benign running commentary, highlighting the good things you're doing.
(See example in the box opposite).

✔ If any difficult feelings come up for you regularly, try be-friending them, chatting with them: ask what you can do to stop them troubling you. See more on this in *Chapters 13* and *17*).

✔ Consider keeping a journal, as a new way of understanding yourself. The book *The Artist's Way* has a good method for this.

Kindly commentary: Alan and the tramp

Alan's walking along a London street, enjoying the bright morning. Then a tramp shambles up to him.

Alan's first response is fear: I don't know how to deal with this guy. Is he on drugs, dangerous?

But Alan tells himself he can handle this, and why not try a small adventure instead of walking on by?

So Alan does well to stop, look the tramp in the eye, and say 'How are you?' In a slurred voice, the tramp says 'Not happy, my mate left me.'

Alan has enough sense to avoid problem solving, and just bear witness: "I'm sorry to hear you're not happy".

And Alan gives him the coffee he'd just bought at a takeaway. He feels he's grown through this adventure.

Remember that the nature of true adventures is that you can't control them, they'll take you somewhere differ-ent, you can't be sure of the outcomes. So let go of any expectations about where you get to with all of this!

Outer adventures

These can include physical activities from the gentlest, like water colours or origami, to the most strenuous. Try to be clear why you're choosing something: be wary if it's just about impressing people, copying others, ticking a box.

The most satisfying outer adventures are probably those which stretch you gently, and in several ways: not just physical fitness, but also emotional resilience, mental skills and awareness. Getting out in Nature can offer all this, and is a classic way to get new insights and direction when you need them.

There are plenty of physical adventures which are flamboyant, brief and expensive, like bungee jumping. You may get more out of quieter, slower, less expensive activities, such as walking or cycling on a pilgrimage route, or doing a vision quest.

The Vision Quest is a classic rite of passage, especially for those entering adulthood, found in native traditions around the world, including Celtic, Norse and Native American. Although details vary, the essence is similar: you spend an extended time alone in one place in nature, for 24 to 72 hours, usually fasting.

Rites of passage for adults becoming elders are more varied and have different names, like the term *Wisdom Quest* for rites of passage which draw from the vision quest tradition, but are tailored to people over fifty.

Social adventures

As we get older, there's a risk that we have fewer friends and personal connections. This may be because people die, fall out with each other, move away, or just simply through retirement. The skills of making and mending friendships become very important in later life, and that's partly what social adventures are about. If you're shy and quiet, you need such adventures even more.

Here are some ideas for social adventures:

- ❖ Try joining one or two new groups. Pick ones where their focus interests you, but deliberately stretch yourself, see if you can make some new contacts, even if it all feels stressful. The book by Dale Carnegie in *Resources* may help.
- ❖ Experiment with turning an acquaintance into a friendship. For example, invite someone you know a bit to join you for a walk or some other outing. Remember, it's an adventure: don't reproach yourself if they turn down the invitation, or your outing feels a bit flat.
- ❖ Do you have any unresolved conflicts in your life? Maybe someone you fell out with years ago, or a person you see currently, who you don't get on with? A brave adventure would be to seek them out, and try to clear the air. Having a third party friend to support you both can be very helpful, and make things safer for both of you.

Many social adventures are a chance to refine your communication skills (expressing yourself *and* listening), and your emotional intelligence (empathy and intuition). Some of the *Resources* for Chapters 2, 3 and 4 can help with this.

RESOURCES

INNER ADVENTURES
▌ **The Artist's Way**
by Julia Cameron
This is now a series of books which can help you discover your creative self, and also have a lovely approach to journaling. Choose the one that suits you best.

▌ **Mindfulness: A Practical Guide to Finding Peace in a Frantic World**
by Mark Williams and Danny Penman.
ISBN-13: 978-074995308-9
The best book I know on this topic: it's a guided self-help process with clear explanations and a CD of guided meditations.

WISDOM QUEST
You can find a longer explanation of this idea in Chapter 8 of my book, *Out of the Woods,* or try this book:

▌ **The Book of the Vision Quest**
by Steven Foster with Meredith Little.
ISBN-13: 978-067176189-9
A beautifully written book by two of the main teachers who have brought the vision quest tradition to a wider audience. It can help you to understand and explore the idea of calling for a dream.

SOCIAL ADVENTURES

▌**How to Win Friends and Influence People**

by Dale Carnegie. ISBN-13: 978-009190681-8

This book was first published in 1936! Its style may seem antique, but there's sound advice on making friends.

Chapter Nine

Afternoon Delights: daily comforts

DO YOU FIND, as I do, that the ageing process is full of contradictions: for example, it's both expansive and confining. You may have more leisure time, more scope for choice, but less energy, less contacts, even less interest in life.

If you're in the Baby Boomer generation, you may just recall rationing after the war, and your parents doubtless had plenty of austerity experience. Even now, my mum at 93 hates wasting food, and so do I. The point of this chapter is to highlight ways to make daily life nourishing for yourself, and drop any habits like 'grin and bear it'.

Give yourself permission

Many of us have deeply ingrained habits, such as duty and austerity, which make it hard to be kind to ourselves. So giving yourself *permission* to ease up, to spend time or money on yourself, is a vital first step.

Several of my friends have struggled with retirement, feeling they should still be 'doing something useful with their lives': in other words, they find it hard to enjoy leisure, lounging around, hobbies, seeing friends and so on. And the idea of spending money for fun is equally hard.

One of my solutions to these problems is to give myself an allowance, a budget, of time and money that's mine to spend as I like. This at least gives some shape to the situation. It can be a good way to deal with demands from your conscience, your partner, your kids, and others.

My aim is to have two days a week where I'm free to do what I choose, daytime and evenings. That's less than 30% of the week, which is surely fair after the decades you've probably been on duty for much of the time.

I also have a guideline that 10% of my income can be spent on enjoying myself. How does this idea sit with you? Growing up in the 1950s when money was tight, even this 10% figure brings up guilt pangs. I manage them by budgeting a larger amount of money to give to good causes.

Nourishing your home

I'm constantly fascinated by how different people's homes are. Some give you a feelgood vibe as soon as you step in, some are spartan or chaotic. It need not take much effort or money to make your home a beautiful, nourishing place for you and others.

Many surveys show the Danes to be the happiest people in Europe and the world, and the quality of *hygge* seems to be one reason. *Hygge*, pronounced *hoo-guh*, is about friendly cosiness. *Hygge* matters most on long dark winter nights, and you'd feel it through candles, snuggly blankets, comfort food and flowers. You can make your home cosier by using more wood for floors, walls, furniture, and bringing nature indoors – flowers, twigs, pine cones, fur rugs.

Rhythms and variations

Daily rhythms can be a good way to give shape to our life, and remind us to relax, enjoy the moment, or whatever other qualities we want to sustain. Here are a few examples:

- → Getting outdoors for some exercise, at least half an hour, most days.
- → Doing a set of yoga, pilates or other indoor exercises to keep you supple.
- → Stopping to enjoy a cup of something (and a bit of cake?), mid morning and mid afternoon.
- → Meditating, maybe at the start or end of the day.

→ Phoning a friend.

→ Play some of your favourite music, every day.

In the same way, small treats or surprises can help you enjoy daily life a bit more. They don't need to be elaborate: you can probably find good ways to surprise a partner, a friend, or even yourself if you're living alone!

Human nature tends to be habitual, so use this to embed simple pleasures and helpful activities into your day. Mindfulness encourages us to savour and enjoy every moment, and it's good to remember this, so habits don't become automatic. Alongside this, try some deliberate variations, do the unexpected, and disrupt your schedule. I love my afternoon tea at four o'clock, but it's good to know I can skip it altogether sometimes.

Composing and flowing

Another way to find daily delight is to try different approaches. You could *compose* some days: create a shape and a plan that will please you, the way a picture or a piece of music are composed. On other days, try being entirely fluid and unplanned: follow your whims, or see what turns up. You'll probably realise quickly that you normally prefer one or the other of these modes – if so, try the other way sometimes.

Several other chapters of this book can help you with daily delights: for example friends (*Chapter 3*), communities (*Chapter 4*), gifts of time (*Chapter 6*), and gifts of inspiration (*Chapter 7*). The habit of appreciation will help make every day more delightful.

Making it special

One way to make everyday life more delightful is to find ways of making something feel special. For example, when I was living alone after my first marriage broke up, I would sometimes invite myself to a beautiful dinner at my own house: cooking good food, lighting candles, putting on some favourite music.

My younger daughter shares my love of afternoon tea, but always makes it seem more of an occasion, by using a table cloth, posh plates, flowery napkins, and her brilliant home-made scones. If you have a partner, setting up treats or special occasions for each other is a great way to enrich the everyday.

RESOURCES

▌ **The Little Book of Hygge: the Danish Way to Live Well**
by Meik Wiking ISBN-13: 978-024128391-2
This is a delightful, comforting guide to hygge, full of yummy pictures.

Part 2

DIGGING THE CHALLENGES

Chapter Ten

Good Vibrations: managing your health

IF YOU'RE IN YOUR LATE sixties or seventies, it's pretty certain that health will be a bigger concern than it was a few years ago. By now, it's probably clear that good health is something you need to work at. Like a vintage car, you probably need more maintenance, and careful handling.

Health is a massive topic: the aim in this chapter is to highlight some basic principles, and sources of help for problems. Much of this chapter is my summary of the fuller Health chapter in my earlier book, *Out of the Woods*.

In recent years, I've seen several older friends who took good care of their health but experienced serious illnesses. Being careful guarantees nothing, but it does reduce your health risks. So the aim of this chapter is both to highlight the basics of good health, and how to prepare and respond if serious illness comes your way.

The first piece of health advice is to begin getting to know, and positively making friends with your body again. For instance, try looking at your near-naked body in a full-length mirror in the morning. Rather than feeling angry or even ashamed about the look of your older body, spend a moment each day having a smile about your appearance, seeing the realities of ageing for what they are, and gently sharing in your older body's way of joking. Your body and you will get on much better if you do.

* * *

Physical exercise: Thirty minutes a day

Here's the bottom line based on the best research evidence: you need to commit two and a half hours each week to physical activity. Making this a regular habit will significantly reduce your risk of developing serious and dangerous illness, such as heart disease, diabetes, asthma, stroke and some cancers. It will also help you to lose weight. You need to do at least thirty minutes of physical activity such as 'fast walking' on five days of the week. This kind of physical activity is called 'moderate-intensity physical activity', and it means doing enough to raise your heart rate and break a sweat. Fast walking and cycling are the most common types of 'moderate-intensity physical activity', but there's also jogging, dancing, swimming, badminton, tennis, etc.

If you have any concerns or worries about how your body feels when you exercise, go to your GP.

Eat well!

Modern eating habits have created a huge number of health problems and illnesses, of which the biggest is obesity. There's also increasing research evidence that having a poor diet significantly increases your risks of serious illness, such as heart disease, stroke, gut (gastro-intestinal) disorders and disease, diabetes, and some cancers, especially bowel related cancers. Food and diet are complex territory, so here's basic advice for which the research evidence is the strongest.

You need to eat at least five portions of a variety of fruit and vegetables per day (a portion weighs 80g). These should be eaten in place of foods which are higher in fat and calories. For example, if you feel hungry between meals, dried or fresh fruit makes a good healthy snack, rather than chocolate or a sweet biscuit.

Important general advice about healthy eating is to eat three meals a day, always have breakfast, and don't skip meals. Skipping meals will just make you feel more hungry, think more about food, and more likely to overeat in the evening or snack between meals.

Lose weight!

The serious health risks of being overweight are the same as for being inactive and having a poor diet, but this time disabling and painful long term physical problems and illnesses such as arthritis, joint problems, and especially bad backs are added to the list of dangers.

So maybe you think you need to lose weight, but here's the challenge – do you actually want to? Motivation is key: take time to explore and develop your personal reasons for wanting to lose weight. Losing weight also requires a systematic plan. Do not do 'crash diets': the research shows that except in the very short term, they don't work. A well planned six-week programme to lose weight has far more chance of succeeding.

Your plan will have much more chance of success if it involves other people. For some, this will be through the encouragement, support and back-up of a partner or friend. Others may prefer to be in a bigger formal or informal group, and there are many different dieting organisations to choose from.

Healthy lifestyle motivation checklist

- *Always take the time to clarify your motivation.* Decide what it is you want to achieve in advance, always be honest with yourself and be prepared to modify your aims if necessary as you proceed. Set off on the right course with the right intentions and you'll have the best chance of achieving your aims.
- *Set realistic goals.* Avoid high expectations that will leave you disappointed. As part of a longer steady journey, taking small steps one at a time, you are far more likely to succeed.
- *Take time to visualize yourself losing weight, exercising, or eating healthier meals.* Imagining and actually picturing positive outcomes and mentally rehearsing can really help you succeed in the actual practice.

- **Make good habits.** Create routines for yourself, and get a bit obsessional about 'same time, same place' commitments.
- **Use your mind as your personal trainer.** Find different ways of sharpening your mental focus and also of relaxing the mind, and this can really help you create a healthier lifestyle. The practice of mindfulness is a good approach (try **www.self-compassion.org**)
- **Learn to be flexible.** It is inevitable that you are going to miss the occasional targets or sessions week by week. Don't beat yourself up about missing a day or two of exercise, or eating the wrong foods, but simply make sure you get back to your routine the next day.
- **Make sure you enjoy yourself.** A healthy lifestyle can be fun, and it doesn't have to feel like a chore. Identify the bits you like and enjoy, note the feel-good moments when they arise, and do more of the things that produce them.
- **Congratulate yourself regularly on the journey.** Whether it's exercising or losing weight, use your achievements for positive reinforcement.

Searching for health information

There are many high quality and free sources of trustworthy health information. One good option is to use online health 'Gateway Sites' as your primary ports of call. Rather than putting the symptoms or illness name directly into a general web search, always go to one of these 'Gateway Sites' first and then do your first searches from there.

The Health on the Net Foundation (**www.hon.ch**) provides a HON Code Certification for health information medical websites and it is a useful kitemark to look out for when searching:

HON @ CODE CERTIFIED 08/2017

Good 'Gateway Sites' will always display this sign.

In the UK, the NHS provides an enormous amount of online information sources. However, the oceans of NHS information are so vast it's not always easy to find what you're looking for. Depending on the general area you are searching, there are two different NHS sites you need to know about:

→ **NHS Choices www.nhs.uk/conditions/Pages/hub.aspx** for information on illness and diseases, dealing with over 800 conditions including all the major serious illnesses, and where to find local services.

→ **NHS Live Well www.nhs.uk/LiveWell/Pages/ Livewellhub.aspx** for healthy lifestyle information and advice (high quality and research based).

A number of registered charities are also health gateway sites, such as **www.patient.info**

On any of these health gateway sites, put the name of your illness or health problem into their search box, or the particular symptom or the name of the disease if you already know it. This will take you to the specific area you need for information. A good idea is to use two health gateway sites and compare the results, say both **patient.info** and **NHS Choices**.

Finding information about alternative medicine can be both confusing and problematic. Try RCCM, Research Council for Complementary Medicine **www.rccm.org.uk** This site is HON Code Certified, while nearly all other complementary and alternative Medicine sites are not. It also has a useful index which explains the various alternative medicine approaches, with links to all their main organisations. These will explain in greater detail about the particular treatment methods, and will usually list practitioners in your area.

Navigating serious illness

Even as you are hopefully living some of your best years in your sixties and seventies, at a certain point a serious illness may strike.

The challenge of a life-threatening illness can also be a potential awakening, both to what you are leaving behind, and to what's potentially available to you through healing and renewal. In fact, being faced with the reality of your own possible dying is your biggest life-affirming opportunity for making your big choices and decisions.

From the time when you first receive the bad news, to finding healing and hope, and the time of your eventual recovery here are three important guidelines:

1) ***Manage your meetings with doctors positively***
   (and with nurses and other healthcare professionals).
   Plan ahead and make sure you always ask your most important questions! Write down the questions: two or three questions each visit are usually about as much as you can cope with in the time and the stress of your appointment. Examples of questions about include:

   - What is the name of my illness?
   - Is there a diagnosis?
   - What is the best treatment?
   - Are there other treatment options?
   - How do I find out more about my illness?

2) ***Organise yourself in advance***
   In advance of a medical procedure, especially if it involves staying in hospital, get organised as much as you can. When you travel you have to think of all the things you need to take with you, and it's the same with a serious illness.

3) ***Find a health advocate***
   Make your illness a "we" experience. Having a companion with you who is prepared to accompany you through thick and thin, who can also speak up for you when you cannot find the words yourself, is probably the single most beneficial thing you can do to help yourself when you are ill.

Be bold when asking somebody for help! From the outset of your illness, try to find somebody close to you who you trust, and you think is prepared to go with you to all your appointments and consultations with healthcare professionals. If you want to talk about the situation with your chosen companion before the appointment, and what you are expecting to happen, this can be a good idea too. If you have written down your most important questions, you can perhaps ask them to write down the answers for you as best they understand them during the appointment. Tell them to write down anything else the doctors or nurses are saying, and give them permission to ask for more explanation if something does not make sense to them.

These trusted health companions in the "we" relationship are often called health advocates. The prime role of an advocate is to support you. Much of this is practical:

- Putting out the call for help among your family and friends and coordinating offers.
- Taking care of the home front, and making sure family needs are not forgotten.
- Speaking with healthcare professionals when you want.
- Writing down your medical history as it progresses.
- Helping to plan and organize everything.
- Setting goals and rewards on your road to recovery.

RESOURCES

Age is Just a Number: What a 97 Year Old Record Breaker Can Tell Us About Growing Older
by Charles Eugster. ISBN-13: 978-075156537-9
A practical, optimistic guide to ageing and health by a dynamic 97-year old.

▌ **The Power of Two: Surviving Serious Illness with an Attitude and an Advocate**
by Gerri Monaghan, Brian Monaghan (2009).
ISBN-13: 978-076115259-0
An inspiring and practical "experience and common sense" book by a husband and wife team in a strong 'we' relationship (he has cancer, she is his health advocate).

▌ **Preventing and Surviving Heart Attacks**
by Dr Tom Smith (2006). ISBN-13: 978-812220267-0
A 'Positive Guide' book for this important topic.

▌ **The Warmth of the Heart Prevents Your Body from Rusting: Ageing Without Growing Old**
by Marie de Hennezel (2011). ISBN-13: 978-190574484-8
A compassionate exploration by a French doctor of the perils and pleasures of ageing.

▌ **Middle Age: A Natural History**
by David Bainbridge (2012). ISBN-13: 978-184627267-7
Explores the science (it's written by a vet) and how best to respond to the physical and natural phenomena of ageing.

▌ **10 Secrets of Healthy Ageing: How to Live Longer, Look Younger and Feel Great**
by Patrick Holford. ISBN-13: 978-074995654-7
A good practical guide to many of the issues.

Chapter Eleven

ALL OVER NOW: HANDLING LOSS

THE AIMS OF THIS CHAPTER are to help you handle losses well, to find their upsides, and feel more robust about the future. Getting older brings more losses to most of us, plus the fear of more to come: but there are ways of learning to grow through this.

Losses at this life stage come in many forms, including death or separation from parents, partners and friends; leaving a job or a social group; or losing some of your own health, energy and talents. This could make you uptight and withdrawn: you may have to make a conscious choice to see loss constructively.

For some people, around 70 is when they face up to their own mortality. It may be many years off, but it's now over the horizon and coming towards you. Later in this chapter we'll consider how facing your dying can enrich your living.

In the best-selling *Book of Joy*, the Dalai Lama and Desmond Tutu speak touchingly of feeling the pain of loss, but choosing to focus more on the openings it can create. For example, the Dalai Lama still misses his homeland in Tibet, but celebrates how his exile has brought him many new relationships and opportunities. This chapter offers some guidelines on grieving as the vital first stage in facing loss, then offers you pointers on how to find the potential opportunities.

* * *

Good grief

All major losses are really a form of bereavement, and most experts believe that we have to feel the pain, grieve the loss, in order to move forward. You can try to deny it, or avoid it by throwing yourself into something new or addictive, but really there is a call to face the feelings and open your heart even to pain.

Elizabeth Kubler Ross, a leading psychiatrist,' suggested that there is a cycle in the grief process: here is a summary of the five stages she identified:

1. *Denial:* This stage occurs when someone refuses to believe that news of a loss, or impending loss, is true. They try to carry on as usual.

2. *Anger:* It is easy for people hit by a loss to be overwhelmed with anger for a while: perhaps at themselves, or the people directly involved such as a spouse who's leaving, or the professionals who might have helped, or at God for letting this happen. Remember that anger often arises when someone is feeling vulnerable.

3. *Bargaining:* This stage is an attempt to make the problem go away, especially typical with a life-threatening illness: "if you take this away, then I will...". It is rarely realistic, and realising it won't work often triggers the next stage.

4. *Depression:* This stage is a collapse of hope that the problem will resolve. It involves accepting that you are human, are prone to illness or death, and that you are in a situation where you have virtually no influence over the event. Depression may be fuelled by guilt: a sense that this crisis could have been prevented if only you had done x. This stage calls for accepting yourself as you are, forgiving yourself and others. Letting go of hope is painful, but it's a prelude to facing reality and accepting it.

5. *Acceptance:* Once you accept that a painful event is happening and you can't prevent it, you have the chance to start to re-invent your sense of self and to seek a positive response.

If you have a loss to grieve, how long should it take? Norms and comparisons don't help here. Learn what works for you. Solitude and privacy can be important, so that you can fully let go into your feelings. Sitting in the pain of loss may seem hard, but it can be very healing. It's quite typical to go back round the five stages described above. So long as you're feeling the emotions fully, you're not stuck. Often the intensity of the present grief comes from the pain of an original wound which was never cleared: now you have a chance to deal with the history.

A good way to finish the grieving process, and to test if you are ready for this, is to consider how you can complete and celebrate what you lost. When my father died, the closest family members had a weekend together, six months after his death, to scatter his ashes and share our memories. It was a lovely completion, which would have been impossible at the funeral, when the grieving had hardly begun.

Hi ho silver lining

When you're hurting from a loss, believing there's a gift in it may feel hard: but seeing this as a chance to grow, heal, and learn can give you the strength and desire to go through the pain. Here are some ideas about possible upsides in your loss:

- *Original wounds and changing the story:* many of us had an early upset which shapes our response to any other loss. A big upside in later life is to change the story we tell about ourselves. See *Chapter 15* for how to do this.
- *Releasing habits:* what are your habits for coping with life's pressures? Maybe escapism, taking it out on someone else, or alcohol. A loss may intensify your habits, but it could help you to notice and change them.

- *Expanding your toolkit:* if loss hits you hard, check what new skills could make it easier. For example, expressing your feelings, making new friends. Several other chapters can help you with this.
- *Reach out:* when someone we know suffers a loss, it's natural to want to reach out and support them. When a loss hits you, try to stay open to this support, to the chance of new connections, and maybe resolving old conflicts. For example, a death in a family is a chance for those left behind to draw closer.

Face Your Dying to Enrich Your Living

We'll drink the wine down to the last –
Drink with the Beloved.
Take this breath like it's your last –
Drink with the Beloved.
We're a caravan you see,
Moving towards our destiny:
You must find the eyes to see –
Drink with the Beloved.

From a Sufi song by Allaudin Ottinger

Do you wonder what's the point of thinking about death? Maybe you're in fine health now, so it seems irrelevant. There's a good reason to consider death now, which is: you can enrich every day of your life by your awareness of death. If you talk to those who work with dying people, or read books like Stephen Levine's, you'll see that many experience dying as a gentle transition, a release. If you find death scary, dig into the reasons: they may just be the general taboo on this topic in our society. If you have real fears, the sooner you can face them the sooner you're free to enjoy life fully. For help with this, see *Resources*.

> *"I'm not afraid of death: I just don't want to be there when it happens."*
> Woody Allen

Can you say that you have faced up to death, in a practical, emotional and spiritual sense? It's liberating to do so. If you have a partner or adult kids, talk to them about your will and your funeral preferences. This helps to normalise the topic of dying: and if you start with practicalities, it makes it easier for you and those close to you to talk about the feelings too. These points can help you start engaging with this big topic:

◆ Look at the animal or plant world – death is a natural part of the cycle. What are your hang-ups about it?

◆ Let go of the illusion that you're in control of your life. In death and life, all you can do is influence, not control, and realising this can bring you to a more realistic two-way relationship with the world around you, and free you from the stress of trying to control everything.

◆ If there are things you want to say to people before you die, do it now. It can enrich the rest of the time you have with them and ensure that you get the chance to do it.

◆ Cultivate gratitude: appreciation arises naturally when you recognise that this moment is all you have, this life could end any time. Thankfulness will enrich your life and others around you.

◆ Live every day as if it's your last: doing this will help you focus on what matters, drop resentments and petty conflicts and apologise where you need to. At a time when my wife Linda and I had relationship problems, this one principle transformed the situation.

◆ Get your admin straight – i.e. will, funeral preferences, papers and financial records.

Life beyond life

What do you believe lies beyond death? Ponder this – maybe take the question into solo time in nature. And ask others what they believe: it can lead to some interesting conversations. If you do believe there is something beyond death – let's call it a life of the spirit – try to contact it now, in this life. If you can feel a connection to the life beyond, it can guide and enrich the rest of this lifetime.

I believe we have a soul that travels through numerous lifetimes on its journey, and which chooses each life it comes into, including parents, partners and other major circumstances. This belief means that instead of feeling like a victim about problems in my life, I say that my soul has chosen this situation and I need to find the gift, the growth point in the problem. If you can see your physical death as a transition, not a total ending, it may help you to face it more positively.

Is this where I get off?

So far, this section is mainly aimed at people whose death is years away. However, some of you may be dying now or facing a life-threatening condition such as cancer. Others may have a partner or close friend in this situation.

This section is the best help I can offer, accepting that it's very different to be in this for real. A couple of times I've had symptoms which could have been a life-threatening illness, but within a couple of weeks the tests cleared me. I've had several friends with cancer, strokes and other potentially fatal conditions: some have recovered, some have passed on. And I've read the books of Stephen Levine, which share his years of experience with people in this situation. My pointers are these:

- Facing death or the possibility of death is usually a shipwreck of life as you knew it. You may risk drowning in bewilderment, confusion and fear. Try to find your centre in this moment, in the heart, in choosing to focus on positive qualities like gratitude, trust and love.
- Stephen Levine comments that patients who meet conditions like cancer by fighting them have more stress and poorer recovery rates than those who meet their health challenge positively, engage with it and learn through it. See his books for more on this.

- ✆ Combine surrender and acceptance that living *or* dying can be okay for you, with a commitment to do all you can to recover your health and get whatever help you need.
- ✆ A spiritual path, practice and teacher can be of huge help to you now: if you don't have one yet, it's not too late to find one.
- ✆ While it may not seem fair, realise that you may have to give some support to a few of those closest to you. I have seen several couples where the dying person was more calm and centred than their partner.
- ✆ You may find that some of your friends can't cope with your condition: it may trigger their distress about things they can't control, their fear of death and so on. If such friends are a drain on you, ask them to stay away.
- ✆ Look for the joys and good bits, however brief and small: appreciate everything you can.

RESOURCES

▌ **On Grief and Grieving: Finding the Meaning of Grief Through Five Stages of Loss**
by Elizabeth Kubler-Ross and David Kessler
ISBN-13: 978-147113988-8
This is a detailed explanation of the five stages of the grief process, and how to use them.

▌ You can also find a summary of the five stages of grieving and more details at **www.facingbereavement.co.uk**

▌ A good website, relevant to handling grief and finding good coping strategies for many kinds of loss is:
www.helpguide.org/home-pages/grief.htm

▌Who Dies? An Investigation of Conscious Living and Conscious Dying
by Stephen Levine. ISBN-13: 978-038526221-7
A beautifully written book which can help you live well and die well. Much of it is relevant at any time in the mature years, and some is specifically about the time of physical death. There are some good guided meditations, exploration of what lies beyond death, and useful lists of books and music.

▌Healing into Life and Death
by Stephen Levine. ISBN-13: 978-094655148-4
This excellent book differs from *Who Dies?* (above) in its strong focus on self-healing, with more of a workbook flavour, guided meditations and exercises.

▌The Tibetan Book of Living and Dying
by Sogyal Rinpoche. ISBN-13: 978-184604105-1
Written by one of the most warm and engaging Tibetan Buddhist teachers, this is a relatively approachable way into the deep and complex Tibetan teachings about conscious dying, the life beyond, and how this can enrich life now.

▌**Dying Into Love:** this website offers some powerful wisdom from teachers with a lot of experience in this area, such as Ram Dass and Joan Halifax. See **www.dyingintolove.com**

▌**Dying Matters:** a UK website raising awareness of dying, death and bereavement. It encourages people to talk about dying, and offers useful advice, contacts for support and links to other useful organisations. See **www.dyingmatters.org**

▌**Die-a-log forum:** this offers compassionate conversations about death and dying via a growing network of Live Groups, a website with a members-only forum, and open access areas for resources and essential information about death and dying. Set up by Max Mackay-James. See **www.diealog.co.uk**

Chapter Twelve

Hold Me:
befriending your fears

IT'S ENCOURAGING TO KNOW that 65-79 is the UK's happiest age group, but this is also a time when fears come up more intensely. You may have found, like me, that ignoring or supressing your fears doesn't help much. The aim of this chapter is to show you some positive ways to handle your fears: to live with them more easily, and learn from them.

To give yourself a positive start with this, think back ten or twenty years: recall your fears and worries then, and you'll hopefully see some progress. Chances are that you've got through some of your old fears, so give yourself a warm hug for that, and realise you have some ability to do this.

If you feel that your fears are getting on top of you, it's probably time to take the initiative. One way is to start with 'what's on top,' the fear that's bothering you most right now. Another, if you're in a robust mood, is to poke around in the shadows, and take stock. Here are some suggestions which may help you:

❖ At your age, you may be challenged by new fears around your health, your looks, the risk of being infirm and dependent, or of dying. Don't panic! Read on.

❖ This is also a life stage where major issues from early life may come up again. For example, if one parent left home when you were a young child, fears of abandonment may recur now. If so, treat this as an opportunity to heal a major pattern which may have shaped your life adversely.

❖ Be aware of patterns coming down from earlier generations in your family, and of key anniversaries: for example I've known many people feel shaky when they reach the age at which a parent died. We can inherit fears that have run through our ancestors, and maybe we've got the chance to clear them.

❖ Check out if some of your fears are someone else's. If a close family member or friend is preoccupied with a major fear, it could affect you too. Likewise, the mainstream media keep pumping out worrying news which can make us habitually fearful.

Find your allies

If you're facing a challenge, it makes sense to call in reinforcements. Allies can be inner or outer, and may come in many forms. Inner allies means finding those parts of yourself that can give you strength, comfort, and wisdom to get your fears into perspective. Looking back at when you've made progress is one way to do this. Another method is to find the various positive inner voices or subpersonalities who can help you: this is explored in *Chapter 17.*

Outer allies can take many forms, including:

- A close friend willing to support you in working with your fears.
- A spiritual guide who you can pray to for support and insight, such as Jesus, Mother Theresa, Buddha, or a Celtic saint like Bridget.
- A place in nature, which you may actually go to, or imagine as a way of feeling safer.
- Someone who helps you professionally, such as a counsellor or therapist.

Next in this chapter we will explore various ways to work with your fears. This can be a demanding and upsetting process. Before you embark on such a session, gather support from some of the sources described above.

Befriending your fears

In this section, we'll explore five processes which can help you face your fears, get them into perspective, and maybe learn from them. You may also find *Chapters 15* and *17* useful: changing the story, and finding different voices and aspects within yourself.

a. Invite your fear for tea. In other words, try to have a relaxed conversation with your fear. You might even try to imagine it as another person, and see how it looks and sounds. Start from a positive belief that your fear is trying to protect you, that it has good intentions, even if you disagree with how it's acting on them.

    Take this slowly, be patient, but really try to enable your fear to find its voice, and to hear it. Taking your fear for a walk in the country may work better than sharing a cuppa.

b. Feel the fear and do it anyway. This is the title of a best-selling booking by Susan Jeffers, which I highly recommend. The following process is mine, but inspired by her books:

Self-help process 3: Befriending your fears

Try this process first on a moderate fear, not a huge one. Begin by telling yourself that you can handle whatever comes your way, and you do have enough strength and support within and around you to do this.

Now, imagine as vividly as you can the situation which scares you. Picture yourself in it, 'feel the fear'. And give yourself time to see yourself finding courage, strength, insight, whatever you need to be okay and come through the fear.

Breathing deeply and slowly can help you stay somewhat calm amid this emotional tension. When you can, start to imagine the outcome you're afraid of, how you could handle it, and keep asking yourself 'then what?' Aim to get to an end point where you feel that you could be okay with the event you fear actually happening.

c. ***Talk with a friend.*** If you have a friend who's resilient and a good listener, there are many benefits in just talking to them about your fear. It's probably best to tell them that you're not seeking solutions from them, just a supportive witness.

You may recall that lovely experience of telling a friend about a problem, and finding that the insights you need just arise in the telling. There may be other benefits in sharing: we may feel ashamed about a fear, we may have an exaggerated view of it, and a friend can reassure us.

d. ***Decrees and Affirmations.*** One reason our fears can have such power over us is that they are deeply entrenched in our brain and our emotional habits. Here are two ways we can use our intent, our will, our conscious power of choice, to reduce this power.

Affirmation: this should be a simple, positive statement in the first person, and in the here and now, which you say repeatedly to outweigh a fear or other negative belief. For example: *I have all the support I need right now.*

Decree: This is a statement in ritual form, where we invoke some higher power within or around us, to support a decree, a statement of a positive condition that we want to displace a fear. Here's an example, tackling fear of abandonment:

In the name of my soul and of Mother Mary, I decree
that I deserve love and loyalty. And so it is. It is done,
it is done, it is done. Amen.

e. ***Enact the tension.*** This is a process I've used with good effect in several workshops. It's another way of having a conversation with your fear, with the help of two people: For this, you'll need two people to help you, a quiet place to do the process, and a good half an hour to include debriefing.

* * *

Self-help process 4: Enact the tension

Beforehand, you as the client need to clarify for yourself the issue that's concerning you, and frame it as a tension between two voices, or two aspects of yourself or the situation. (For example, should I move house or stay here?).

When your helpers are with you, explain that you want them to embody two sides of a difficult situation for you, but to do so intuitively: don't give them any briefing on the situation at all.

Ask your helpers to stand facing each other. You can give each person's role a name, e.g. Yes and No, or Stay and Go. Now, ask your helpers to stand silently, looking into each other's eyes, and start to open to any feelings or thoughts which arise.

After a minute or two, tell your helpers they can move but not speak, and observe what happens.

After another couple of minutes, tell your helpers they can speak to each other: just observe anything they say, don't join in or respond.

When you feel the process is complete, ask your helpers to stop. All three of you should share your experience of the process, with you going last. Then ask your helpers to return to their usual identities, and thank them.

RESOURCES

▌ Feel the Fear and Do It Anyway
by Susan Jeffers. ISBN-13: 978-178504112-9
A great, practical book which helps you do what it says in the title.

▌ Creative Visualisation
by Shakti Gawain. ISBN-13: 978-188003262-6
A short book with a lot of good methods, including affirmations.

Chapter Thirteen

ALL ALONG THE WATCHTOWER — DAILY UNCERTAINTIES

IF YOU COMPARE your average day now with five or ten years ago, is it easier or more demanding? For most people, everyday life is getting more uncertain and complex, and it's not likely to ease up. That's why the skills of *resilience* are becoming so important. Resilience means the ability to handle challenges positively, to grow through them instead of sinking under them.

I've been exploring and teaching about resilience for the past five years. This chapter offers you some of the best methods I've learned or devised, to help you stay happier amid life's uncertainties. As we get older those uncertainties do increase, so the skills to respond well become really important.

> ### Learning from Boiled Frog Syndrome
>
> If you put a frog in cold water and slowly bring the water to the boil, the frog will boil to death. If you drop a frog into boiling water, it will jump out.
>
> Can you see the parallel for humans? Because daily life is gradually getting tougher, we may not notice that we need to change our reactions and learn new skills.

There may be some deep-seated reasons why life feels tough for you: if so, several other chapters may help, such as *11* and *12* on losses and fears, and *Chapters 15* and *17* on changing the story, and finding different voices or aspects of a situation.

* * *

Your resilience toolkit

Resilience is about thriving and staying happy, even with uncomfortable levels of challenge and change. To do this, you need your own personalised toolkit: a set of quick methods that help you to handle stress and problems more easily. Different methods will suit different people: here are some ideas to try out. Practice applying them with milder problems, so you can easily use them if a big wave hits.

A. Relax and get centred

1. *Relax your breathing...* next time you feel tense, notice your breathing. It's probably short and shallow. Taking deeper, slower breaths is one of the easiest ways to feel more calm and centred. And simply giving your attention to your breath should reduce your focus on anxious thoughts in the mind.

   Start by noticing by how your breathing is now, without changing it. Then focus your attention on the lower belly, below the navel, and see if you can direct several long, slow breaths down here. Try pausing briefly after the inbreath and after the outbreath, to slow things down further.

2. *Focus on your body:* this is one of many useful methods known as mindfulness. Under stress, we identify with our anxious thoughts and emotions. Giving your attention to your body and physical sensations is a quick way to calm down. Here is one method you could use:

   Do this exercise sitting or lying comfortably. Start by slowing your breath and focusing in the lower belly. Then slowly move your attention right through every part of your body, starting with the toes, and finishing with the top of the head. Wherever you direct your attention, imagine breathing into that part of the body, and notice all of the physical sensations. If your attention wanders, don't fret, just bring it gently back to the body. At the end, be aware of the body as a whole, accepting all sensations, both the pleasant ones and any which feel uncomfortable. This whole process should take 10-15 minutes.

B. Nourish yourself

3. *Have a healthy treat:* it's easy to use unhealthy habits to cope with stress, such as caffeine or alcohol, smoking, or getting cross with other people. Aim to develop a healthy habit to help you when you are tense. You could try one of these:

Listen to your favourite music	*Play with a pet*
Drink a fruit juice or herbal tea	*Watch a comedy*
Take a long bath	*Go for a swim*
Hug a friend	*Take a walk*

4. *Be nice to yourself:* do you criticise or blame yourself for problems? We often judge ourselves harshly, but it only makes things worse, for ourselves and those around us. Notice your habits, and try to change them. Give yourself credit for trying your best. Focus on what you're doing well. Remember the good things about you, and what other people like you for.

5. *Happy memories:* when you're tense, a nice way to calm down is to remember a time when you felt really happy. Picture it as vividly as you can: the memory can be really cheering and calming.

6. *The blessings of nature:* time in a quiet natural setting can be calming, energising, inspiring and more. Try to do this regularly, and relax enough to take it all in! Even if you live in a city, find a favourite tree, or pot plant. Doing relaxation breathing or other exercise out of doors is extra helpful.

7. *Call a friend:* you might do this either for real, or in your imagination. Actually phoning or meeting up with a friend is calming, it could help you to talk about what's stressing you, and you can ask them for some support or appreciation.

8. *Just imagining a friend can be helpful too:* picture them in your imagination, remember good times you have had together, remind yourself what they like about you, and imagine them next to you right now, supporting you.

C. The 5-step Calmer

This is a quick way to calm yourself down if you are stressed or upset. It's worth learning these five simple steps by heart, and practising them, so you can use this anywhere, anytime you need to. It's not going to solve everything, you may need more time and more help. But it should take the edge off your upset, so you handle problem situations better.

Self-help process 5: The 5-Step Calmer

1. Get centred: take several long, deep breaths. Feel your feet solid on the ground. Say to yourself "I'm letting calmness in". Imagine breathing in calmness, breathing out your upset.

2. Happy picture: Remember someone or something that's positive in your life: maybe a family member, a friend, a pet, or a favourite place.

3. Sympathy and kindness: feel sympathy, kindness and goodwill from your heart, for yourself and the other person/people in this difficult situation. Believe you're all doing your best, and you all deserve kindness.

4. Change the story: Imagine you are playing a positive role, in a story where this 'problem' leads to a happy outcome. Sometimes we make a situation worse by fitting it into a negative story that we repeat (such as 'People always let me down'). Choose a positive story, such as 'I can handle this well', or 'I am good enough'.

5. What do you need now? Try to get clear what you need, here and now, to feel happier. Maybe it will help to tell the other person how you feel, and be heard. Maybe you just want some quiet time alone. Say what you need, and trust that somehow your need can be met.

Learning from Nature

If you think about a garden, an organic farm, or a wood, these ecosystems are remarkably resilient in the face of storms, drought, pests and more. I've spent many years exploring how people can learn from nature about resilience and wellbeing. See more in *Resources* below.

RESOURCES

▌ **Find your Power: A Toolkit for Resilience and Positive Change**
by Chris Johnstone. ISBN-13: 978-185623050-6
Chris is one of my favourite teachers on this topic, and I highly recommend his book.

▌ **The Endorphin Effect: A Breakthrough Strategy for Holistic Health and Spiritual Wellbeing**
by William Bloom. ISBN-13: 978-074994126-0
A useful book which helps explain the physical factors in wellbeing.

▌ **Mindfulness: A Practical Guide to Finding Peace in a Frantic World**
by Mark Williams and Danny Penman.
ISBN-13: 978-074995308-9
The best book I know on this topic: it's a guided self-help process with clear explanations and a CD of guided meditations.

▌ **www.naturalhappiness.net**
On this website you'll find resources I've created to help you learn about resilience from nature, workshops, and info about my forthcoming book *Natural happiness: the Gardeners Way.*

* * *

▌ **Action for Happiness** have a lot of excellent material on their website relevant to wellbeing and resilience, as well as local groups and other events. See **www.actionforhappiness.org**

▌ **Network of Wellbeing** offer some great resources via their website, including videos by experts.
See **www.networkofwellbeing.org**

Chapter Fourteen

Matthew and Son: work and money

YOU MAY SEE WORK as a necessary chore, and be keen to retire; or you may see it as a valuable way to fulfil your talents. Money may be a vital resource to you, or you may not think about it, hoping something will work itself out for you.

Whatever your views, the years before and after seventy are likely to bring big changes in how work and money fit into your life. The aim of this chapter is to offer you some pointers and tools to explore these changes, recognising that people will have widely different views and needs on these topics.

Redefining work

Charles Handy is both a management guru and a holistic thinker. He was among the first to predict the huge changes in our ways of working in the past twenty years, and he coined the term portfolio working. He suggests that work is like savings: it's unwise to invest everything in one place. The notion of a linear career, a steady progression in one line of work from school leaver to gold watch at sixty-five, is pretty obsolete, but what's to replace it?

Handy suggests that we think of work as any activity with a productive output, and aim for a portfolio of work, so we have diverse sources of income and satisfaction. This should also mean that if one piece of our work portfolio disappears, we're not up the creek. In his book, *The Age of Unreason*, he writes of five types of work for the portfolio:

- **Wage work**. *Where money is paid for time inputs.*
- **Fee work**. *Where money is paid for results delivered. This is more typical of self-employment, growing rapidly especially as more jobs are outsourced.*
- **Homework**. *Includes cleaning, repairs, caring for kids or parents: rarely paid, but still vital.*
- **Gift work**. *Voluntary, unpaid work helping others, e.g. in your local community.*
- **Study work**. *Includes training and learning for new skills: growing in popularity as change speeds up.*

One great benefit of looking at your work as a portfolio is that you have several choices to consider, not just one. You probably have various needs from your work, such as money, social contact, learning and fulfilment, and you may look to different parts of your portfolio to fulfil these.

Handy believes the idea of retirement has become obsolete, and I agree with him: the portfolio makes it easier to see your work as a transition across time. As you get into your late sixties and seventies, you may no longer have the energy, desire or financial need to spend as much time earning money, but you'll probably still want a work portfolio of some kind.

I strongly share Charles Handy's view that it's healthy to define work more widely, and to keep active in some forms of work well into our seventies and beyond. However, you may prefer to retire fully, or feel you have to, due to redundancy, health, or other reasons. Your experience of work may be largely as a grind, a chore, a means to earn money. If so, I urge you to challenge your beliefs. Imagine it can be a way to learn, explore, fulfil yourself, and it's never too late to start.

Some work organisations may be reluctant to hire older people, but charities and voluntary groups are a great way to try out something new, and gain experience that could enable you to earn money too. So how might you want your work to be different as you approach and move past 70? Here are some pointers:

❖ Use the portfolio approach, and aim for a lot of flexibility in the hours you work. Make sure you don't get run-down, and have the scope to take time out for treats and emergencies.

❖ See how your work (or parts of it) could help you to develop and use the skills of an elder. See more on elderhood in *Chapter 16.*

❖ If solitude is an issue for you, focus towards work where you're in a team, and have good social contact and support. Conversely, if you need more solo time, focus work that way.

❖ Aim to avoid work decisions being driven by financial needs. *See below for advice on reducing your income requirements.*

❖ Believe that (most of) your work can be fun and fulfilling. Be willing to change and experiment till you get there.

Handling retirement or redundancy

These words may sound threatening, but they don't need to be. The removal of the compulsory retirement age leaves individuals with a lot more choice. Although the idea of redundancy may feel grim, the actuality can be pretty positive. Many people have taken voluntary redundancy as a good way to leave a job where they were stagnating and made a fresh start. Whether you've chosen redundancy or retirement, or had it imposed on you, there are emotional impacts, practicalities and new choices to consider. Let's look at each of these in turn.

Emotional impact

Leaving a job and a work team is a loss and a kind of bereavement, even if you chose to leave and even if you weren't enjoying the job. There will be a hole in your daily life where work and colleagues used to be. Give yourself time to adjust and process it, let yourself grieve and also celebrate, hopefully with the colleagues you're saying goodbye to.

You may feel excited or nervous about having a big space open up in your life. Having freedom of choice can be hard, especially if you're not used to it. It's striking that many people suffer depression, ill health or addictions after they leave work. So recognise that this could be a difficult time and prepare for it:

- ❖ Create a bit of structure, at least for a transitional period: for example, sign up for a weekly adult education class, do one day a week of volunteering or join a regular sports group.
- ❖ Schedule a few treats in case your mood needs lifting: a holiday, an outing or a visit to friends.
- ❖ Make sure you have a good network of friends, so you have mates to talk to and go out with and support in case you need it. If you don't have many friends outside your work, try to change this before you leave.

Practicalities

Both retirement and redundancy are major financial events: it's important for your stress levels to look at this before you stop work, and go through the implications with a professional financial advisor. Make sure that the process has been handled correctly by your employer and that you're getting your entitlements. For example, an employer is usually required to consult with workers before any redundancies. Another important practicality is knowing what State benefits you may be entitled to after you stop work. These are complex fields, where you may need to spend some time researching them yourself or getting help. See *Resources* for more on this.

New starts

Looking back over the decades of your working life, have you enjoyed them most of the time or have they been a dull blur? Do you feel you made good choices or bad ones about the work you did? Or maybe no choices because you were a helpless victim of fate at every turn? Your beliefs are crucial to your future: if you believe you make lousy choices or always end up unhappy in your work, you probably expect the same in future.

If you're carrying this kind of emotional baggage along with you, invest some time in reshaping your beliefs and freeing up your future. *Chapter 15* can help. I share Charles Handy's view that we never really stop work, we just change the forms it takes. And embracing the idea of working for little or no money can be liberating: for a start, it makes you think what else you might want to receive for the energy you put out!

Getting clear with money

Do you have issues around money? Most of us do. Money is such a big thing in our lives that your attitude to money may mirror basic beliefs about yourself. For example, if you often feel short of money, does this reflect a belief that no one values you, you're not good enough or you have to struggle for everything?

Do you have problems about money in your relationships or with your boss? Dig deeper to see what it's really about: perhaps you are competing to get enough love, power or recognition, and finance is simply the currency you're measuring with. Although your money symptoms, like serious lack of it, may look bad, don't start here: use the money pressures to get down to root causes, clear the old emotions, and change the negative habits and beliefs.

"I still don't know if I have money or if it has me."

Peter Koenig, one of the best teachers on money I know, says there are far more taboos on disclosures about money than about sex in our culture. Think of your friends and work colleagues: you probably know a lot more about their personal life than you do about their money. Because of these taboos, you may not have much awareness of your beliefs and habits about money.

One common belief about money is *poverty consciousness*: a sense that there isn't enough money to go round, that you don't deserve to have much. Maybe you believe it's morally wrong to have money, or you shouldn't be richer than your parents, or having money will provoke jealousy and hostility from others. This may link to believing that you can never get enough of whatever you need – money, love and more. There are also people who struggle with having wealth, who feel guilty because they have more than others, who don't know how to balance spending on themselves with giving money to help the starving millions and the rainforest.

Whatever your emotional baggage about money, invest time to lighten the load. You need to reach a stage where your decisions about money are led by clear thinking and a code of values you've chosen, not by floods of muddy feeling. When you believe you're getting towards this level of clarity, use the practical tips below.

Practical tips on money

People's needs, attitudes, and supply of money will vary hugely at this life stage. Here are a few practical pointers which may be helpful. These are tips on a very large iceberg of information. See *Resources* for more.

> £ *Lower your break-even.* This means reducing your outgoings so that the minimum monthly income you need is less. Ways to do this include moving to a smaller house so you free up capital or reduce your rent or borrowings; paying off debts, especially credit cards; making lifestyle choices which mean you spend less, such as selling your car and joining a car club. There are several benefits to this strategy: one is that you have more freedom and power of choice, since you don't need so much income. And a less expensive lifestyle will almost certainly be more environmentally sustainable.

> £ *Plan how to meet your long-term money needs.* Take a thorough look at your needs and wants for money through to the end of your life, and plan how you are going to meet them. You may need more information and expert help to do this, but it's up to you to take the initiative and ensure it's done well. Include in this plan provisions for medical costs and residential or home care.

£ *Understand your future income sources.* The pension field is complex, but you need to know what should be coming to you from pensions and other investments. Although it's a delicate subject, clarify if you're likely to inherit money from your parents or others.

£ *Shop around for good advice.* Finding impartial, objective financial guidance is hard. Many advisors, even those who seem independent, may have ties or bonus payments that distort their advice. You need to invest time to find the good advice you need: ask friends, do a web search, and interview at least three potential advisors. And ask direct questions about how they make their money, what happens to commissions on investments they recommend, and so on. Beware of 'magic bullet' money-making schemes which seem too good to be true: they are!

£ *Plan ahead for family needs.* The biggest may be providing for your partner in case you die first. There are some simple steps which help, like putting assets in joint names, and an accountant or solicitor can advise on these. You may feel you're not providing enough: do what you can and talk it through openly with your partner. If he or she is worried, you could decide jointly to save money now to provide more.

£ *Balance your needs and the bigger picture.* Try to find a fair balance in allocating your spending among different demands. You want to live comfortably, but can you share some of your income to meet the needs of other people or the many problems we have on our planet? In doing so, don't just give money away blindly: have some connection with the people or projects you are helping.

* * *

RESOURCES

For topics around work, retirement and redundancy, it's worth doing a web search as there may be new websites and changes in funding arrangements.

WORK

▌ **Out of the Woods: A Guide to Life for Men Beyond 50**
by Alan Heeks. ISBN-13: 978-184528512-8
The chapter above is a much shorter version of *Chapter 4* from this book, which includes more on all these topics, plus a process for re-visioning the kind of work you want to do.

▌ **The Age of Unreason: A New Thinking for a New World.**
by Charles Handy. ISBN-13: 978-009954831-7
Charles Handy is one of the most perceptive writers about the world of work and its relationship to human needs. This book introduces the portfolio concept mentioned above, along with Boiled Frog syndrome and more. Several of Handy's books have useful insights: for example, *The Empty Raincoat: Making Sense of the Future* (ISBN-13: 978-009930125-7) has a section on the issues of what he calls the Third Age, which is the life stage of the over-sixties.

▌ **What Color is Your Parachute? A Practical Manual for Job-Hunters and Career-Changers**
by Richard Bolles. ISBN-13: 978-160774147-3
It delivers what it says in the title: encouraging and very practical. There's also lots of free information and guidance on **www.jobhuntersbible.com**

HANDLING RETIREMENT OR REDUNDANCY

▌ The website **www.redundancyexpert.co.uk** is a good place to start on many aspects of redundancy: for example, it can brief you about your employer's obligations, how to fight a redundancy, what benefits you are entitled to and also handling depression.

▌ Brilliant Retirement: Your Practical Guide to a Happy, Healthy, Financially Sound Retirement
by Nic Pelling. ISBN-13: 978-027372327-1
It does what it says on the cover: it addresses all the issues highlighted in my short section in more depth, plus others.

▌ Rebuilding Your Life After Redundancy: The New Life Network Handbook
by Janet Davies. ISBN-13: 978-184549101-7
This gives basic coverage to some of the issues and devotes much of its attention to ways to get back into work, including self-employment, volunteering, consultancy, working abroad and others.

GETTING CLEAR WITH MONEY

▌ When you are at the stage of understanding and clearing negative beliefs around money, Peter Koenig's work is very helpful. There's valuable information and useful tools on his blog **www.peterkoenig.typepad.com**
His book, *30 Lies About Money: Liberating Your Life, Liberating Your Money,* ISBN-13: 978-059529236-4, is a short and powerful exposure of some of the commonest misleading beliefs about money.

▌ At the practical level, e.g. looking at pensions, care costs, etc., there are a number of useful UK websites.
You could try the following: **www.saga.co.uk www.giddylimits.co.uk** and **www.mabels.org.uk**

Part 3

FRESH MAPS

Chapter Fifteen

WON'T GET FOOLED AGAIN: CHANGE THE STORY.

ONE OF MY biggest insights since turning 60 has been the way repeating stories shape our lives. The older we get, the more of a limitation our stories become, and the harder it is to change them. If you dig into your worries about your seventies, it's likely that a Story is fuelling them.

So what do I mean by a Story? Most of us have one or two major repeating, difficult patterns in our life. We may not be aware of them, we may not call them a Story, but they really shape our experiences. Most often, a Story begins with a major upset in childhood. Our subconscious mind tries to explain and justify that first upset by repeating the situation. See *Paula's Story* in the box for an example.

> ### Paula's Story: Men always put you down
>
> When she was a young child, Paula remembers how her Dad was angry and dissatisfied with her Mum, on the rare times he was home.
>
> Paula's Dad left altogether when she was six, and her Mum became depressed and unsupportive. In adult life, Paula's partners put her down and left her repeatedly, and she had similar bosses at work.
>
> By her late sixties, Paula had a long history of depression, but eventually realised she was repeating a Story she could choose to change.

This kind of Story is not logical: it's usually not even something we're aware of. It's a primitive survival tool from early years. If you're still repeating a Story like this in your sixties or seventies, it will be a deeply ingrained habit, and you'll need a sustained effort to shift it.

You may know about neural pathways: old habits become physically imprinted within our brain, so they truly are hard to change. But the payback to doing so is that it can transform the way you handle old age.

A repeating Story takes away your power of choice, and means that you don't see situations as they are, because you're unconsciously shaping them to fit your Story. Changing a major life Story is unlikely to be instant, and you may do well to get professional help from a counsellor or therapist.

Most of us have at least one major Story, and some minor ones. For example, look at your beliefs and habits around money, or food, or health. The Self-help process opposite is designed to assist you in seeing and changing your Stories. Try it on a minor one first.

Easing the bumps

Minor, everyday challenges and even major ones can have an upside. They're another chance to identify your Story, or to practice changing it. If you've already named your Story, sometimes you'll realise you're repeating it, while it's happening. Try taking a few breaths, taking a loo break, any way to give yourself a bit of space, and see how you can do things differently, in the here and now.

Often our relationships have a Story too: especially with partners, family, close friends and work colleagues. You can use the Self-help process opposite for these situations too. It can also work for groups, such as a whole family or a work team.

If you can see a Story between you and someone else, what can you do about it? At minimum, you can get clearer how your behaviour causes the Story to repeat, and try to change it. If you're feeling calm and brave, and there's good rapport and trust between the two of you, try actually naming the Story to the other person.

If you can do this, present it as simply your impression, ask them what they think. Even if they have a different view, you'll have learned something and deepened your connection.

Self-help process 6: Changing a Story

Set aside at least 40 minutes for this process, and find a quiet time and place where you won't be interrupted.

Take some long, slow breaths. Make sure you breathe out fully. Let yourself relax.

Now start to remember a few significant experiences in whatever aspect of your life you've chosen to explore, or for your life as a whole.

If this is distressing, keep breathing deeply, aim to witness the emotions and let them go.

Now start to look or listen for a pattern, a repeating feeling or Story. Give this time, be patient and receptive. If nothing comes up, go back over the scenes again.

What you're aiming to find is a simplistic, sweeping statement that feels horribly powerful to you, and probably makes you tense up. A good sign that you've found it is words like *always, never, can't, no good.*

Be very gentle with yourself, don't blame or judge yourself for carrying this Story for so long. Be grateful you've found the courage to name it and face it now.

The next step is to find an antidote to your Story: a simple, positive statement that you can affirm whenever the negative beliefs come up.

Here are some examples of negative Stories and an affirmation (positive statement) as an antidote to them:

- *Men/women always let me down: I fully deserve love and loyalty*
- *I'm just not good enough: I always do my best and deserve support*
- *People never respect me: I have all the strength and safety I need*

It helps to repeat frequently the affirmations you've chosen. And if something upsets you, use the situation to see what Story it's showing you. Trust that you can change your Story, and choose a happy one.

If you can find agreement, you've got a powerful way to improve the relationship. In my fifties, I recall a stormy period with a girlfriend where we'd regularly pause in mid-argument, and say "we're doing it again!"

Happy endings

People love stories: it's how we make sense of life. So remember, the aim is to *replace* a negative Story with a positive one. A negative Story is often what underlies and fuels the fears we're aware of, so if you can start to choose and affirm a positive Story, it can have big benefits in many parts of your life. Look for a simple, hopeful statement which lifts your spirits, is easy to remember, and which you can repeat to yourself often. It will raise the prospects of a Story with a happy outcome!

Chapter Sixteen

Something Tells Me I'm Into Something Good – exploring elderhood

DO YOU REMEMBER the naïve joy of that Herman's Hermits song?

> *I walked her home, and she held my hand,*
> *I knew it couldn't be just a one night stand.*
> *So I asked to see her next week, and she told me I could:*
> *Something tells me I'm into something good.*

That simple optimism may seem far away at your age, in a world so complex. The fresh map offered in this chapter might help you find some sense of a steady, positive centre, through elderhood. The term elder is used with various meanings: I'm using it to invite you to connect with the mature wisdom in yourself, and in our ancestors. Traditional tribal cultures, such as the Native Americans, Celts, and Bedouin, had great wisdom, including the role of the elders.

We may think of tribes as led by one chief, but often the elders as a group had a powerful role. It was their role to guide the tribe in a crisis, to dream dreams, uphold values, and mentor the young. Clearly we live in a different kind of society to this, but the role of the elders is something we can learn from and update.

* * *

Here's one pointer:

> *There is, it seems to us,*
> *At best, only a limited value*
> *In the knowledge derived from experience.*
> *The knowledge imposes a pattern, and falsifies,*
> *For the pattern is new in every moment*
> *And every moment is a new and shocking*
> *Valuation of all we have been.*
>
> T. S. Eliot

I've concluded that each of us has to figure out our own form of elderhood, and what being an elder means for us. This is different from the tribal traditions of initiating adolescents into adulthood, where they are told their duties, roles and values. Initiation into elderhood is a more organic, gradual, self-guided process. You may learn from other elders as role models, they may give support, but the vision comes from you, and any guiding spirits or divinity you work with. The point of the T. S. Eliot quote is that elderhood isn't just about experience: it's how you can use that to face the unique qualities of here and now. Here are some of the best ways to explore what elderhood means for you, and to move into it.

- Alone and in nature.
- Sharing your exploration with others of your own age, in a regular group or one-off events.
- Using dreams, meditation and other practices which help you open to the spiritual and the unconscious aspect of yourself.

When does elderhood begin, and finish? Everyone's journey is unique. The age of 50, 60 or 70 can be a turning point. However, I've seen people with the wisdom of elderhood in their late 20s, and others in their 70s who've not yet reached it. I believe that elderhood is a stage we find for ourselves, hopefully in our 60s or 70s, and this stage of elderhood lasts until we die. There are others who see elderhood as followed by seniority, a stage of passing out of life and into death and whatever lies beyond.

To help your exploration, here are some brief pointers to aspects of elderhood:

- **Simple presence:** if you're at ease with yourself, calm amid setbacks, focussed on the positive, your presence alone will be a teaching and a role model for those around you, of all ages.
- **Embodying and upholding values:** this is a major role of tribal elders, and much needed in our society. It means living the principles you believe in, such as honesty, integrity, forgiveness, and speaking out for these values when you see them ignored.
- **Elders as a group:** in these later years, the balance between individual and collective life swings more towards the group: this means shared wisdom, mutual support, and perhaps shared action too.
- **Friendship:** slowing down should be a goal and a benefit of elderhood. This creates time for you to be a friend: to other elders, to your children and grandchildren, and wherever it's needed. Sharing your love, your wisdom, your values with others through friendship is part of your legacy.
- **Giving back, serving the greater good:** this is part of living your values, and creating a legacy.
- **Facing ageing and death:** I was closest to my father, and learned most from him, in his last years and his death: I know many others who have found the same. If you can find happiness even in your decline, and face death positively, you create a blessing for yourself and younger generations.
- **Surrendering to the unconscious:** if you have stayed aware, you probably feel by now that the complexity inside and around you is so huge that you can't think your way to understanding. Surrendering to the unconscious is not giving up, it's opening to receive the wisdom within us and around us, which can't all be channelled through the rational mind.

❦ ***Opening to the beyond:*** the years of elderhood are a chance to open to the world of spirit, to whatever lies beyond death. This is a fitting part of our later life, and probably serves the tribe as well.

There are so many pressures pulling people and governments around the world towards the immediate, visible problems, which are often social and economic. Raising attention, speaking out, walking the talk, calling for action, on the huge but less immediate crises of environmental and human sustainability, is a role that the elders need to take up. The elders are a big voice, a power for change, and without us stepping in, we're all on the road to hell.

RESOURCES

▌ **Four Quartets**
by T. S. Eliot. ISBN-13: 978-057106894-4
This long poem contains a lot of wisdom about life, and elderhood in particular.

▌ **Out of the Woods: A Guide to Life for Men Beyond 50**
by Alan Heeks. ISBN-13: 978-184528512-8
This book covers many of the topics in *Not Fade Away* in a lot more depth. Chapter 11 is an extended exploration of elderhood.

Chapter Seventeen

Listen To Me:
different voices

ONE OF MY FAVOURITE insights on ageing is from Carl Jung, the great pioneer of psychology. He observes that in early adulthood we select a few of the many voices within us to be our adult self. In middle and later life, we either open the door to those other, ignored voices, or they break in through the window.

Within each of us there are many aspects, voices and sub-personalities. The ability to hear more of these voices and integrate them into an expanded sense of self can help you grow into a fuller, mature version of yourself. This chapter will offer you a couple of ways to contact and learn from different aspects or voices within you, and in Resources you'll find ways to get further help with this.

There are many processes which can help you access these voices: some of them name the voices you might look for, such as the Inner Judge, the Magical Child and so on. These can be useful, especially if this approach is new to you, but you can simply choose to start listening and create your own map: See *Self-help process 7* overleaf.

 Some voices will be a kind of inner recording of people who have influenced you. If one of your parents was controlling and judgemental, you may find their exact words coming back from the Inner Judge.

How can this approach help you? Often our inner airspace is hogged by a few voices that keep grabbing the microphone, with a negative message. This is one way that unhelpful habits and patterns entrench themselves.

For me, the Hurt Child alternating with the Inner Judge ('*You're no good, you don't deserve any better, told you so*' etc.) has been a strong negative force in me for decades, and it has taken hard work to get airtime for the positive voices. It doesn't help to suppress or ignore the negative voices: better to accept them, help them, but don't let them run the show.

The quieter voices can expand your sense of who you are, and give you confidence and fresh solutions. I once had an amazing dream which I called Clapton and the Hermit. It showed me two major voices in me that seemed to conflict with each other. The Eric Clapton voice wanted me to be famous and admired; the Hermit just wanted a quiet life in the woods. Then I had the stunning insight that I could be both: I could alternate between the limelight and solitude. Both voices could be heard and satisfied.

Self-help process 7: Inner listening

In a quiet, safe space, get comfortable and take some long, relaxing breaths. Let your mind clear, feel yourself open and receptive. Invite any inner voices to speak to you. Welcome them, give them a hearing. After a few minutes, ask if there are other voices that want to speak. Invite your higher self to talk to you. Ask for advice on issues you are facing. Complete by thanking all these voices for their help.

Take a few minutes to digest your session: it may help to make some notes. If you repeat this process several times, it should deepen and you will receive a wider range of voices. You can ask the wiser voices to speak directly to aspects of yourself which are pained and confused. Sometimes you may find two voices in conflict: for example, one wanting to stay with a job or relationship, and the other wanting to leave. If so, ask other voices for their perspective and ask your higher self to arbitrate or give you an overview on how to proceed.

Voices in action: Martin's story

Martin grew up with a bullying father who always told him he wasn't good enough. His mother was a timid woman who never stood up for herself, or him. In Martin's mid-fifties, his father died suddenly of a heart attack. When I met Martin ten years later, he had emerged from several years of depression, and voice dialogue with a counsellor's help had been the catalyst.

The first inner voice I found was the Fearful Child, and soon after, the Angry Father. I had taken in all my father's putdowns and they justified my low achievement in work, my failed marriage and lots more. Slowly I found the Higher Self, and a voice I call the Kind Elder, which has echoes of older men who have given me support and good advice over the years.

Now I could start to converse with the Angry Father. I realised he was trying to protect me from further attacks and failures by keeping me on my toes. He was frightened, exhausted and needed my sympathy. Then, I began to hear the Magical Child, who had been squashed early on. It was healing and exciting to find a part of me that wanted to enjoy life, and could do so at my present age. Another voice which slowly emerged was the Good Mother: not my actual mother, but the way I wish she had been. Now I give myself some nurturing and I can accept it from my current girlfriend.

Working with a counsellor at first was invaluable for me. I wasn't used to this kind of thing, and in some sessions a lot of distress and anger came out that needed clearing. Now I can do the process for myself. If I get upset or have a problem to sort out, I make some time and convene a kind of internal meeting.

Who's in there? Surprises!

Discovering whole new aspects of yourself can be exciting and unsettling, like meeting family members you'd never heard of. This process takes time and courage: you may find that the old dominating voices resist, telling you this is rubbish. Try to negotiate with them, acknowledge their fears but ask them to support your wishes.

Self-help process 8: Exploring your chakras

It's best to do this process lying down, in a quiet place where you won't be disturbed. Allow at least an hour for it, begin with some long, slow breaths to relax. Then start with the base chakra. Give the whole process plenty of time: if you don't get to all seven chakras, you can always do another session.

Base chakra: This energy centre is located at the perineum, in the crutch – it's sometimes called the *root chakra*, and is associated with the colour red. This centre can connect us with basic issues of physical safety and survival. Breathe deeply into this centre, and listen for a voice that can express any needs or issues to you.

Sacral chakra: This centre is located in the lower belly, below the navel, and is associated with the colour orange. This part of the body connects with our sexuality, and may hold deep, difficult emotions like fear or shame.

Solar plexus: This centre is in the middle of the solar plexus, and its colour is golden yellow. Here you may connect with issues of power and vulnerability, and how you project yourself with people around you.

Heart: This centre is located in your physical heart, and is associated with the colour green. Through this chakra you can explore deep emotions, such as love and grief.

Throat: This chakra is located where the chest and neck meet: its colour is turquoise or light blue. This centre can connect you with your voice in the full sense, including how you express yourself (or not), and with artistic creativity.

Brow: This centre is in the middle of the forehead, and is sometimes called the third eye. Its colour is dark blue. Here you can explore your mind, your will, and your judgement.

Crown: The crown chakra is on the top of your head, and its colour is white. Through this chakra you can connect with your higher self, with inspiration, sense of purpose and with the spiritual realm: what some would call their guardian angel.

The hidden voices you find can be very different from your public personality: eccentric if you've been conventional, analytical if you've been creative, quiet if you've been exuberant, and vice versa. There may be some small, hurt pieces of you hiding fearfully since childhood that need comforting. Women may deepen contact with their Inner Man, and men with their Inner Woman.

Exploring your chakras

This is another way to explore different voices within yourself. Chakras is an Indian name for a set of energy centres within us: physical parts of the body which can connect us with different issues or faculties. This may sound a bit esoteric, and there are whole books on the subject. The simple approach I'm describing here is one I've used for myself many times. (See *page 110* opposite)

It may take a few sessions before you start to hear the voices of all seven chakras. Visualising a physical location and a colour for each voice can help you contact some deep, hidden strengths and challenges. You can evolve this further by imagining a gathering of all the chakra voices in a circle, so that they can talk to each other.

This was how I realised that my mind (the Brow chakra) was highly critical of me generally, and this was holding me back in how I related to people, and my sense of power (the solar plexus).

RESOURCES

▌ **Embracing Our Selves: The Voice Dialogue Manual**
by Hal Stone and Sidra Winkelman. ISBN-13: 978-188259106-0
Although published back in 1989, this is a classic in its category.

▌ **Voice Dialogue:** There are books, workshops and individual therapists using this method. See **www.voicedialogue.org.uk**

▌**Family Constellations:** Don't be misled by the name. This is a powerful method to explore aspects of yourself and to clear relationship issues within your family, work team or friends, developed by German therapist, Bert Hellinger. There are many different websites for Constellations therapists.
Try **www.movingconstellations.com**
Ask friends, or do a web search on 'Family Constellations UK' and see who feels good for you.

Chapter Eighteen

My Generation: wisdom from others

THIS CHAPTER offers you the personal experience of a variety of people around ageing. Many are from people I know personally, plus a few that I've picked up in my research. I hope they give you a fuller sense of how differently people can experience getting older, and what possibilities it offers.

A view from age 67: Steve

Steve is an American friend of mine, still working part-time as a well-paid consultant, and enjoying his second marriage.

Ageing: I don't really think about it. I sure don't worry about it. I've had some minor health problems, I've dialled down on my work schedule, but my focus is just to enjoy life right now. Laura and I are doing our best to spend the kids' inheritance: they can look after themselves. We want to travel and enjoy the good life as long as we can.

A view from age 69: Charlotte

Approaching seventy, later this year, has been wonderful and I have never been more comfortable in my own skin. Or in my soul. I am enormously privileged to have enough money, time, good health – all key to the good life – and I sense that we may be the last generation for a while to be honoured with all three. Maybe the many blessings of getting older are a well-kept secret in a youth-obsessed culture.

There has been a definite shift towards a deepening commitment to my inner life. The gap between who I am on the inside and who I am when facing outwards diminishes each year. I have no patience for small talk, pomposity, inflated self-importance. Achievement is less and less relevant, while the relationship people have with themselves, the world and humankind is ever more important. The close relationships I have are marked by quality over quantity, and the time I spend with family and friends is authentic, nourishing and nurturing. 'Spiritual friendship', both one-to-one and in a group of older women, is an increasingly important aspect of my connection with others. I choose to live on my own, and solitude is bliss, in the knowledge that I am well loved.

It is still a challenge to allow myself to surrender to a new way of being, with less emphasis on the doing. Service to others is at the core of who I am and how I pass my time, but is it distracting me from something more urgent? Is it ok to not be busy and useful all the time? And if I'm not busy and useful, who am I? And what's the point?

My three score years and ten in July will be marked by two events. I am planning to donate a kidney to an unknown person – I don't need two – and I shall be running an ultra marathon of 40 miles through the night. I took up running three years ago, and for me it encapsulates an enthralling interrelationship between body, mind and spirit.

Life is still an adventure, and each new year inspires, surprises, and tests me. Gratitude is a precious gift. I try and avoid giving advice but if asked for one top tip for those approaching their later years, it would be to live as truly as yourself as you possibly can. Do your life your way. For if not now, when.

A view from age 71: Gay

At the age of 60, Gay had the courage to uproot herself from a close-knit community in Cambridge, and join me and four others to co-found a co-housing project in rural Dorset, the Threshold Centre.

Staying happy in your seventies

Be proactive in caring for mind, body and soul. For me this begins with daily yoga and meditation practice. Be ever open to new experiences and ideas. Keep the brain working in whatever way is best for you. (I learn the words to happy/positive songs and sing them out loud to myself during the first few challenging hours of the day.) Keep a relationship with nature, even if it is only a plant in a pot. Cultivate gratitude for all the blessings in your life.

How has turning 70 been?

Turning 70 was fine. I couldn't believe it in a way – I kept having to redo the maths to convince myself this huge number related to me. I really like being an 'elder'! The tricky one for me was turning 50 – neither one thing or the other.

What has helped?

Being the oldest in this community. Giving myself permission to grow old disgracefully when I choose, and gracefully when I want. Giving myself a 70th birthday present of a tattoo, and having red and purple highlights in my hair. Being made to feel very special on the day by my co-housing neighbours with bubbly and presents and then sharing a Mad Hatter's Tea Party with another friend celebrating 50 years.

Any advice to those approaching 70?

Spend as much time as possible with people younger than yourself. Honour what you can do rather than worrying about what you can't. Laugh as much as possible, particularly at yourself. Have a party and celebrate. Learn something creative and non-physical. I never picked up a paintbrush till I was around 60 and it is now the greatest joy in my life.

A view from age 74: Giles

Giles is a long-standing friend of mine, who despite keeping fit and active has had several life-threatening health crises since his early sixties.

Advice to those in their sixties

- ✔ Delegate to others more than you think you can safely do! You can't do it safely. How did you learn? Don't delay this!
- ✔ Get out into nature and meditate, pray, ask questions of yourself – you are god or whatever you call that thing.
- ✔ Recognise crises as invitations to break through old patterns, beliefs and views. They are milestones to be celebrated and a good crisis should never be wasted. You now have the wisdom to deal with any chance or any shit that comes your way.
- ✔ Let go of stuff you are holding onto. For each self-imposed manacle released, there will be a boon.

How did you feel approaching 70?

Getting a hit of my teenage thoughts about the absolute improbability of being around in 2012, more the century and the year than the idea of being 70.

I had been retired for a year, but had planned that as a gradual process over 6 years, so it was not the dramatic cross-roads many experience. On the other hand, I have been just as busy in the 4 years since, but the nature of my busyness has been increasingly moving away from the preoccupations of the previous 30 years of "work life" and been more mellow than busyness.

A fuller appreciation of my partner of 42 years and my 5 sons, through calmer listening, not acting or speaking out every urge or thought I have. For me a key challenge has been to let go of having to be useful. Another has been to avoid having an unrealistic agenda of things to do – most of them are unnecessary, can be given to others or massively simplified.

If only!

What has helped my transition to the seventies

- ✔ Talking to young people about absolutely anything they are interested in.

* * *

✔ Putting heart before head to a greater extent in deciding what to do this minute, this hour, this year or for years ahead. This is truly liberating, often adventurous and always energising.

✔ My sons – vitality, different takes on life, their love.

✔ My wife – her changing wishes as to how our partnership works as each of us accept and pursue personal change, whether physical, mental, emotional or, combining all, spiritual.

Staying happy in your 70s

It's the people and the truth and love you bring to dealing to them ALL that count, not your or their appearance, behaviours, plans, status, achievements etc.

A view from age 74: Sara

It is not my line to 'transit' from one state to another: rather I am me, progressing. It all stays with me; always there in the bundle to meet what comes to me 'in the moment'. There is no differential in 'moments' up until I die: although they will all be filled with different things. After I die I know not what will happen.

Loss? Sadness? Carried from earlier times, yes. But losses change shape, starting from younger days when lost things had to be absolutely replaced, to knowing that they are really illusory. I can occasionally still hear the howls of sorrow from inside, but with compassion more than pity.

Rage? Yes, about things done to me and by me. Rage is a good mover and cleanser, but it is exhausting and distracting and needs to be passed by. But I have recently learned to show my rage for my sake, to cleanse me and pass on. What a relief. It happens less and less. Disguise and pretence and other hiding mechanisms can also be dropped. I am much more likely to notice them now, and can kindly pass them by in myself and in other beings.

Clarity is so simple and helpful and joyful and is the essence of this time of consolidation in my life. I have invented enough. From

50 until 74 I have realised more and more the blessing of long and lengthening family and friends. I have now accepted what I have provided myself with. I love to think, analyse, and just be. I have adventure, and inquiry, but also stillness and content. Old patterns of problem maintenance are being spotted and are more and more discarded with a kind pat. The stuff in my back pack is mine, not other peoples. And now is now: so be not afraid.

A view from age 76: Rita

Rita was my host for a night on a pilgrimage in Italy. She lives alone in a tiny cottage, and at age 70 started to open her house to pilgrims.

Turning 70 was a beautiful time – I had been letting go from my life since age 40 everything that wasn't essential, and now I felt clear. I had a near-death experience at 40 – I chose to come back to be of service, but was still seeking to know how/what, and I keep seeking, but I'm at peace with it all.

A view from Age 81: Becoming 'Middle-Old'

Marian Van Eyk McCain

Marian is the author of the book 'Elderwoman', *and has explored these issues for herself and with others for many years.*

Seventy wasn't a major transition for me. In my sixties I was building an eco-house, growing veggies and writing books and the seventies simply felt like a delightful extension of the sixties. I was healthy, fit and energetic, still walked several miles a day and still grew veggies. I believed old age was going to be like that all the way to the end and if I went on eating healthily, exercising, meditating, enjoying good relationships and having lots of meaning in my life I was going to maintain this same feeling of physical and mental wellbeing and wholeness, right through to my last breath.

For me, the crunch came at eighty – remarkably, shockingly fast. I suddenly *felt old*. I started to notice stiffness and weakening in my joints, new aches, tremors where there had been none, doubts where there had long been certainties. Now I was making mistakes, forgetting things, forgetting words and names and feeling ashamed of it. I found myself losing efficiency and losing motivation.

I started to feel a sense of diminishment, as though bits of me were falling off and more and more were going to fall off until I was stripped down to my bare essentials—whatever those were. I knew my task was to make spiritual sense of all this—because I had always been able to make spiritual sense of life stages—but suddenly I didn't know how and the challenge seemed too great. Yet answers always come, once you have faced the questions. And I have absolute faith that some day soon I shall be writing with assurance about this transition too. Right now I'm simply facing the question.

All I know so far is that the transition from 'young-old' to 'middle-old' is a big one. (Researchers define 'middle-old' as 75-85.) As Piaget pointed out, although life stages don't happen at the same age for everyone they always happen in the same, predictable order. So for all I know, someone else's seventy milestone might have similar qualities to my eighty milestone. I think it's the same transition.

When Bill Plotkin wrote, in *Nature and the Human Soul*, about the last two life stages (The 'Master in the Grove of Elders' and 'The Sage in the Mountain Cave') he was not old himself so he relied on in-depth interviews with just two people: Joanna Macy and Thomas Berry. We need lots more people to share their experiences of becoming 'middle-old' and 'old-old' (over 85). Especially those who have already embraced these later stages and have something to share. We need to find the answers together. Pioneers all, we need to map this new territory and help those who come after us to navigate its tricky trails.

If I was mentoring someone in the young-old (65-75) life-stage my advice to them would:

✔ be sure to revel in being in such a potentially full, powerful and fulfilling phase of your life and treasure every moment of it.

✔ look forward with fascination, like an explorer, to noticing and studying your own ageing process, how it feels, how it unfolds.

✔ make sure you have at least one friend of a similar age – or better still a group – to swap notes with.

✔ things can change fast so monitor carefully, now, what new projects you take on, especially those that involve long commitments.

✔ be aware that no matter how all-absorbing your outer life is now, in time it may gradually start to be your inner life that feels most important to you.

A view from age 82: Dr Peter Fenwick

Peter Fenwick is a neuropsychiatrist who works with several hospitals, and has written several books, including 'The Art of Dying'.

Old age gives us an opportunity to examine our lives, to look back and see the context of the life we have lived. Visiting old friends and parts of the world we have yet to see can help this process.

It is crucial to accept that you are going to die. Try getting a map of the process and decide what sort of death you want, including making a Living Will and planning music for your funeral.

As the prospect of death draws nearer we need to look more closely at who we are. This means aiming for non-dual consciousness, not our existing subject/object consciousness with our ego still attached to life. I suggest the website for Sailor Bob Adamson, which will help you find who you are.

www.sailorbobadamson.com/videos

Sailor Bob advises you to recognise the naturalness that you are – pure, all pervasive, space like, ever-expressing, spontaneous presence-awareness.

Next, it is important to clean up our lives, and a first step is to forgive ourselves, then those who have hurt or offended us, resolving any outstanding conflicts and mending family rifts. An extraordinary example is Lester Levenson, who was given a diagnosis of terminal heart failure, and in the few months he believed he had left realised that love was the source of his happiness and resolved to spend the time sending love to all the people he knew and had ever known. By doing this, by clearing negativity from his life, he not only gained remission from his heart failure but transformed himself, 'awoke' and entered full consciousness.

All the evidence we have from the dying suggests that we have no need to fear it. How do we die? The work of Monika Renz about the dying process shows how people experience a new reality very much like the world of the near death experience, full of light, love, compassion and feelings of unity. They often describe a 'waiting area' where they may see spiritual beings, and often their own dead relatives will be present. This new realty is experienced by 90% of the consciously dying.

Such transformative experiences suggest that a patient has completed their journey and may be comparable to a spiritual awakening. Monika Renz identifies three stages in the dying process: pre-transition, transition and post-transition. It is essentially a process of surrender and letting go of the ego and moving into a non-dual consciousness where one experiences a spiritual opening and a sense of peace.

A view from age 92: Norah

These days it's commonplace to live into the Eighties, which for most of us has become a bearable decade, sometimes – optimistically – called today's Sixties. Reaching ninety shatters that pretence. Time and space become tighter and more precious. My old nanny at the age of 98, said "I don't have much future but I do enjoy the present." This also means that one cannot plan very far ahead – I was reluctant to pay a deposit on a cruise in six months' time in case by then I'm a late rather than an early bird.

After ninety, I had to get serious and summarise the ultimate lessons of my life's journey, keeping only the truly essential ones. I found only two. One is to disidentify totally from the body, which has been my vehicle since birth, but has now become an invalid friend whom the rest of me, my non-physical essential self, has to carry and cope with. The other is to enjoy every new day but be ready to die, with acceptance and deep gratitude. Having had the great gift of an out-of-body experience in my youth, teaching that my body and essential self were two separate entities, I look forward to repeating it.

Chapter Nineteen

Woodstock: a festival for the 70s

By the time we got to Woodstock,
We were half a million strong,
Everywhere there was song and celebration.
Joni Mitchell

IMAGINE THIS CHAPTER like a festival, a gathering of music, movies, books to celebrate the adventures and the grungy bits of getting older. Wander round the festival site, and see what takes your fancy. Feel the excitement of so many others on this journey with you. I've organised this festival rather simplistically, by categories. Within these you may find light and funny, serious and insightful, and mixtures of both.

MOVIES

Le Weekend: This is one of the best films about ageing, and about relationships in midlife. It shows the intense contradictions of many long-term couples: the shared jokes and familiarity alongside fierce resentment, the dependency mixed with an urge to break free and change, so that staying together or blowing apart both seem obvious *and* unthinkable.

Nick and Meg are a Guardian-reading couple from Birmingham, on a long weekend in Paris to celebrate their thirtieth wedding anniversary. The film is a kind of extended conversation between them, with a huge, brilliant and convincing spectrum of moods and roles: from deadly argument to tenderness, from shared joy in the moment to solitary paired despair. There was a resonant murmur from the (oldish) cinema audience when we see Nick bopping and singing, badly but with feeling, to early Bob Dylan on his iPod.

The Best Exotic Marigold Hotel: Marigold Hotel is a clever example of fiction anticipating fact. With so many other labour-intensive services being outsourced to India, why not retirement living? The film's basic plot is a varied bunch of English over-50s trying to live in a rundown hotel in Jaipur which is trying to serve 'the elderly and beautiful'.

This country takes everything to extremes: beauty, pollution, spirituality, overpopulation. The different ways in which these English oldies adapt, or fail to, are really entertaining and instructive. Just being in Jaipur is a shipwreck, and the ways they re-invent themselves are remarkable. The Indian characters are just as vivid as the English ones, and their influence on each other is beautifully observed. I loved the scene where the retired judge gives the street kids tips on batting technique, and ends up playing cricket with them.

Being somewhere so different forces a level of honesty, and urgency, which all of us beyond 60 would do well to adopt. Death and sickness are such visible parts of the everyday in India, that it forces you to value being alive, today. This pushes two of the film's sixty-somethings through the usual barriers, and into a playful, even youthful romance.

One of the odd things about being beyond 60 these days is its lottery quality – like the uncertainty of who's got money, and who hasn't. This film gives a sensitive picture of the shame and lostness of middle-class people suddenly finding they're broke at retirement because of dud investments.

Hope Springs: Early scenes paint a poignantly convincing portrait of a couple who share a house, but not much else. They have been in separate bedrooms for years. Arnold (played by Tommy Lee Jones with echoes of Jack Nicholson) is in a boring job, and spends his evenings watching golf programmes on TV until he falls asleep.

His wife, Kay, is brilliantly played by Meryl Streep: we can see traces of the younger, beautiful Meryl we remember, but Kay is overweight, lonely, with her self-confidence erased by years of her husband's indifference. At one point she says, "I'd feel less lonely if I was actually living on my own."

The real turning point is when Arnold realises that unless he changes, the marriage may well be finished. And once both parties really want to change, it seems that trying a little tenderness does the trick.

Song for Marion: The film's focus is an elderly couple, played to perfection by Vanessa Redgrave and Terence Stamp. One of the delights of this movie for us oldies is to see two great stars still in their prime as they themselves get well into old age.

Like me, you may remember Terence Stamp as Sergeant Troy in *Far From the Madding Crowd*. Here, as Arthur, there's a powerful mix of character, strength, and decay. Arthur has clearly spent most of his adult life in anger, resentment, and deep fear of opening up to others.

Marion, played by Vanessa Redgrave, is Arthur's wife: she loves him as he is, and makes his life viable: for example, she's the one who keeps the family talking to each other. As her health declines, we see one of the classic shipwrecks for older men: Arthur has depended on her social skills, and without them, he digs himself deeper into isolation and depression.

One of the few times we see Arthur cheerful is on his weekly night out at the pub with a few male friends. But he doesn't know how to reach out to them, and vice versa. Arthur's recovery from the shipwreck arises from unexpected sources, which I won't reveal.

Amour: Stunning is a word much over-used, especially by estate agents, but stunned is the best way to sum up my feelings at the end of this film. I have never seen a whole audience leave a cinema in such deep silence. The gist of the plot is easily described: George and Anne are a cultured French couple in their eighties, living happily in their Paris apartment. Anne has a minor stroke, and then a major one: George devotes himself to caring for her.

Before you stop reading this for fear of depressing yourself, it's important to say that there's a lot of sweetness in this film. As Anne loses her mobility and her faculties, we really see the love between the couple deepen, and George keeps finding her where she can be met: singing a children's song together, or a touch of the hands.

However, it's not an easy film to watch. We see how George's own life evaporates, as all his attention goes on Anne. We see how demanding, and how lonely, this care can be, and how such situations can be divisive within families.

FICTION: BOOKS AND POETRY

The Dark Flood Rises
by Margaret Drabble. ISBN-13: 978-178211833-6
She turned 70 recently, and wrote this book to explore ageing. It weaves the stories of several characters with quite different beliefs and experiences – it's a good story, as well as illuminating and thought-provoking.

The Tempest
by William Shakespeare. ISBN-13: 978-185326203-6
This was Shakespeare's last play. Its central character, Prospero, is believed to be semi-autobiographical and to express a lot of Shakespeare's own feelings about later life. The play starts with a physical shipwreck, an imagery that runs through the play, along with exploration of how to create a new life. A great play to read, and even better in live performance.

The Essential Rumi
by Rumi and translated by Coleman Barks.
ISBN-13: 978-014019579-8
How could a medieval Persian poet still be a best-seller in our times? Rumi has wisdom and sweetness for every stage of life and death.

* * *

Here's an example:

The Guest House

This being human is a guest house.
Every morning a new arrival.

A joy, a depression, a meanness,
some momentary awareness comes
as an unexpected visitor.

Welcome and entertain them all!
Even if they're a crowd of sorrows,
who violently sweep your house
empty of its furniture,
still teat each guest honourably.
He may be clearing you out
For some new delight.

Four Quartets
by T. S. Eliot.

This is my favourite poem, and it has a huge amount of wisdom about life in general, and ageing. For example, its exploration of how we experience time, and how we seek to make sense of our life, are brilliant. Be patient: you may have to read it several times to digest its rich, dense eloquence.

All Passion Spent
by Vita Sackville-West. ISBN-13: 978-086068358-2

Whilst the central figure is age 88, I strongly recommend this to baby boomers, because it can give you a positive view of late old age, and a road map towards it.

The central figure is an 88-year-old widow: the story begins just after the death of Lady Slane's husband, Lord Slane, a dry but distinguished figure, who in his time has been Viceroy of India and Prime Minister. Their children are mostly a ghastly crew, in their sixties, who assume that Mother will now live with each of them in return for rent.

To their amazement, Mother, who they see as an unworldly simpleton, takes a stand, and tells them she intends to move out to Hampstead. The children grudgingly offer to come all the way to Hampstead to visit her, but she replies:

> *"I am going to become completely self-indulgent. I am going to wallow in old age. No grandchildren. They are too young. Not one of them has reached 45. No great-grandchildren either; that would be worse. I want no strenuous young people... for it would only remind me of the terrible effort the poor creatures will have to make before they reach the end of their lives in safety."*

Desert Wisdom: A Nomad's Guide to Life's Big Questions from the Heart of the Native Middle East
by Neil Douglas Klotz. ISBN-13: 978-145651647-5

There are many ways into the spiritual realm, and this is a brilliant book for people of all ages and genders. There is immense diversity of insights, approaches and methods to explore, including the original truths of Christianity, Islam, Genesis, Sufism and other sources.

Testimony of Light: An Extraordinary Message of Life After Death
by Helen Greaves. ISBN-13: 978-184413135-8

It's hard to decide if this book is fact or fiction. It is written as a description of the afterlife, described by a dead nun to her still-living friend, Helen Greaves. Is there an afterlife beyond this human one? If we knew more about the afterlife, could that guide our human life here and now? This book offers some of the most convincing answers to these questions that I have found.

Reading this book made me realise that my images of the afterlife are flimsy and simplistic: a Heaven and Hell, loosely derived from the Old Testament, plus a bit of karma dogma from the East. Whereas Frances Banks describes a more subtle, encouraging afterlife, much closer to the original teachings of Jesus as explored in the work of Neil Douglas Klotz.

MUSIC

Mervyn Stutter: Songs for Menopausal Flower Children.

This is a brilliant CD, with lyrics that find the humour and poignancy of being an ageing baby boomer, set to the tunes of Sixties hits. For example, you may guess that The Menopausal Soldier is a skit on The Universal Soldier. Very funny, and evocative. He has two other CDs, and does a great live show.
See **www.mervynstutter.com**

Your favourite Sixties music:

I really urge you to dig into your memory banks or vinyl collection to recall the songs, groups, lyrics that meant most to you in your youth. You may learn about who you were then, and find it's still part of you now. For example, this song from The Doors meant a lot to me then, and still does:

> *People are strange, when you're a stranger,*
> *Faces look ugly, when you're alone.*
> *Women seem wicked, when you're unwanted,*
> *Streets are uneven, when you're down.*

And one of my comforting antidotes was *Summertime* by Janis Joplin:

> *One of these mornings you're gonna rise up singing*
> *And you'll spread your wings and you'll take to the sky...*

Brahms: Sonata No.1 for Cello and Piano:

For me, this beautiful music says a lot about the journey into later life. The low deep sound of the cello seems to express qualities of elderhood: at times quite slow and reflective, but rising into the lyrical, helped by interplay with the brightness and wider musical range of the piano.

Eric Clapton – 461 Ocean Boulevard:

I've followed Eric's music and turbulent life story since the very early days (remember John Mayall, or the Yardbirds). I admire the way he's faced his difficulties, and enriched his music through them. Seeing him live, you can see sense that all his feelings are pouring out through the guitar. I'm especially fond of this album: it shows how the blues can uplift us, and how a song can be a prayer, as in *Give Me Strength*.

Sing with others:

If you've never been part of a singing group or choir, give it a try! It's a wonderfully uplifting, companionable thing to do with others. Check out Harmonic Temple groups as a way to start.

NON FICTION BOOKS

The Warmth of the Heart Prevents Your Body from Rusting: Ageing Without Getting Old
by Marie de Denezel. ISBN-13: 978-190574484-8

One of the best books I've found on ageing: especially useful for the young-old, who, as Marie observes, are often terrified of being old-old. This is a positive, practical guide to enjoying life at any age beyond fifty.

Emotional Intelligence: Why it Can Matter More Than IQ
by Daniel Goleman. ISBN-13: 978-074752830-2

This is written for men and women of any age, but it addresses a key need in later years: how to become emotionally articulate in the inner life and with others. To live happily and working with emotional dynamics is far more important than mental IQ.

New Passages: Pioneering Second Adulthood: Mapping Your Life Across Time
by Gail Sheehy. ISBN-13: 978-000255619-4

This is a brilliant overview of the sequence of life stages which most people go through, with the differences for men and women, and insights on how to face them more easily, including the later stages.

The Virginia Monologues: Why Growing Old is Great
by Virginia Ironside. ISBN-13: 978-014104371-5

She's best known as an agony aunt: part of the fun with this book is how she owns her own blind spots. Virginia was 65 when she wrote this, and its focus is on the sixties, not turning seventy. However, it offers a good, easy-to-read mix of wry humour and occasional insights.

Chapter Twenty

I CAN SEE FOR MILES: FUTURE OUTLOOK

IT MAY SEEM ODD that many people think more about the future as they get older, but it's appropriate. In tribal societies, one role of the elders was to dream into the future, and share their insights to guide the group.

In recent years, I've felt an urgency about understanding the outlook ahead, and what we can do to face it well. Most people find the pressures of here and now are growing, and they don't want to think about the future. This is understandable. In many ways, our brains and bodies are tuned to the life of primitive hunter-gatherers, handling what's in front of us. Research shows that humans are poorly equipped to face up to large, complex, long-term possible threats, which is why most of us blank out about climate change and lots more.

Why is it worth pushing ourselves to look at the future, when it's hard to do? Because you have some power to improve the outlook, and to grow your resilience if you make it a priority. And because you can play a traditional elder role in sharing your insights with the people around you. In this chapter, we'll share a process for facing the future; we'll look at some of the threats and upsides ahead; and we'll explore realistic ways you can share a more positive outlook.

* * *

Deep ecology: a way to face the future

If you're working with hazardous materials, you need good methods and equipment. The future really is hard to face: it can easily feel bleak and overwhelming. Many people feel pain and despair about the state of the world and the environment, and blank out to avoid these feelings.

One of the best processes I've found for facing this pain, and moving on to face the future constructively, is called *Deep ecology*. It's been evolved by an American teacher, Joanne Macy. She writes:

> *"...The energy expended in pushing down despair is diverted from more creative uses, depleting the resilience and imagination needed for fresh visions and strategies. Fear of despair erects an invisible screen, filtering out anxiety- provoking data. In a world where organisms require feedback in order to adapt and survive, this is suicidal."*

Her approach combines the science of ecology with nature-based spiritual teachings from Buddhism and the Native Americans. Joanna Macy has a clear, simple method to help us face the big issues and find our ability to act on them. In summary, these are:

1. *Opening to gratitude*
2. *Owning our pain for the world*
3. *Seeing with new eyes*
4. *Going forth*

She explains that this is a four-step cycle which we need to spiral round repeatedly: it's not a one-off transformation. Let's explore each step in more detail:

 1. *Opening to gratitude.* Whatever your challenges and worries may be, try shifting your focus to thankfulness: for the gift of life itself, and all the resources that keep you alive. Include the many gifts of Nature, such as food and

beauty, and the good things you receive from other people: friends, family, and the huge array of workers we all depend on. Starting with gratitude helps us be present in the here and now, to relax and open up beyond our worries.

As Joanna Macy says: *"Thankfulness loosens the grip of the industrial growth society by contradicting its predominant message: that we are insufficient and inadequate. The forces of late capitalism continually tell us that we need* **more** *– more stuff, more money, more approval, more comfort, more entertainment."*

2. ***Owning our pain for the world.*** This stage can be tough: it helps to find a group or mentor to start it with. Macy's books contain excellent methods to help you do this, both alone and with others. Most of us stuff down and deny the pain we feel at the ways that the earth and its creatures are being abused and destroyed. It takes courage to face your pain, it can be distressing, but this step should enable you to move into the next two.

3. ***Seeing with new eyes.*** By letting yourself feel your pain for the world, you open up to a new sense of connection with that world, and with other people. Macy calls this *"a shift in identification... from the isolated 'I' to a vaster sense of what we are."* This is a crucial prelude to the fourth step. As small, solitary egos, we may feel powerless. When we feel ourselves as part of the living network of life, and part of a community, something different becomes possible.

4. ***Going forth.*** This is the stage of taking action: maybe as an individual, maybe with others. Macy describes this as *"the discovery of what can happen through us... one simply finds oneself empowered to act on behalf of other beings – or on behalf of the larger whole".* And taking action includes holding a vision of positive change. See more below.

A look ahead: bad, worse, better

Exploring the future, and how to respond to it, has been a major part of my work for several years. I think our view of the future reflects our temperament: if you're usually optimistic and relaxed, you'll trust that the future will sort itself out okay. If you're naturally anxious, as I am, the future will give you plenty of cause for alarm.

In this section, I want to share some of the outlook for the UK, as I see it, based on views of various experts. In the following section we'll explore what you can do. Before you read on, I recommend that you work through the four-step deep ecology process above.

Think of significant increased pressures in the past 5-10 years, and imagine them increasing a lot further:
- Political and economic disruption through cyber-attacks (as in the last US Presidential election).
- Further growth in refugee and migrant movements.
- Major and minor terrorist attacks in developed countries.

Now add some new pressures:
- Major rise in food prices, and occasional supply shortages.
- Frequent cyber-disruption of daily activities (banking, internet, mobile phone use).
- The 'culture of cuts' leads to a significant rise in disruption from strikes, walkouts, and protest actions, by both workers and service users (e.g. NHS patients, commuters).
- The NHS have to make major policy decisions on priorities, e.g. cease life-extending treatments for anyone over 80.
- Technological innovation become more radical, and seem to have a life of their own (driverless cars, genetic modifications, artificial intelligence).

Now look at the upsides:
- You are not alone. There are quite a few networks looking at these issues, many with local groups.
  See *Resources* for more.

- The UK has a lot of resources to improve its resilience, if directed well. This includes natural resources, skilled people, and basic services and infrastructure.
- There is a good track record of the UK innovating and coping under pressure: The Second World War is just one example.
- There can be a gift in the problem: See below.

Whatcha Gonna Do About It?

Do you recall the song with this title by the Small Faces, in 1966? The spirit of the 1960s is worth invoking at this point: especially the sense of possibility, the feeling of collective power when we get it together, and the idealism, the passion for love and peace.

I do believe the future will bring a lot more pressures and turbulence, but I also believe there's an upside. Try imagining that these negative trends could actually move us in a positive direction, look for the invitation, the gift in the problem. Here's my best guess at the opportunities:

❖ Grow your own resilience even more than the pressures. (See more in *Chapter 13*).

❖ Take full responsibility for your wellbeing, don't depend on the system, the State, or other people.

❖ Strengthen your connections with other people: relevant networks, family, neighbours and colleagues: we're all going to need more collective support and capabilities.

❖ See this as a helpful wake-up call, to reduce your time and dependence on 'screen world' (smartphone, social media, etc.), and focus more on local, face-to-face, real personal contacts.

❖ Explore the power of practical vision and positive dreams: See more overleaf.

* * *

You may say I'm a dreamer, but I'm not the only one

John Lennon's words from *Imagine* remind us to have the courage to dream, and to remember that our hopes are shared by millions. Dreams, in the sense of inspiring visions, and myths, in the sense of powerful beliefs, have a huge influence on our world. Think of Mandela and Gandhi: two lone figures whose dreams overturned myths which upheld a powerful Establishment.

A writer who's helped me to see the power of positive dreams is the eco-philosopher Thomas Berry. In his book *The Dream of the Earth* he writes *"we could describe our industrial society as the addictive, paralysing manifestation of a deep cultural pathology…"*. Berry believes humans need to reconnect deeply with Nature, both to give us the insights to move forward, and the passion to act on them and preserve this planet where, in truth, we are *"a species among species"*.

Berry has a sense of optimism about the future, which may seem surprising. It arises from his sense of the intelligence of Gaia, the spirit of Planet Earth, and a belief that if Gaia allowed humans to create this mess, it must be a huge growth opportunity for both humans and the planet:

> *"the basic mood of the future might well be one of confidence in the continuing revelation that takes place in and through the earth. If the dynamics of the universe… guided us safely through the turbulent centuries, there is reason to believe that this same guiding process is precisely what has awakened in us our present understanding of ourselves and our relation to this stupendous process."*

It's important to take actions to face the future, but our dreams matter too. Picture a happy, resilient, sustainable future in as much vivid detail as you can, picture it often. Look for groups where you can feel a shared hopeful vision, and also pray for what you hope for. Who knows how positive tipping points come about: let's do what we can.

RESOURCES

▌ **Scanning our Future:**
This is the project I set up in 2016 to research future pressures, and ways to raise our resilience to thrive in the times ahead. See more at **www.futurescanning.org**

▌ **Active Hope: How to Face the Mess We're in Without Going Crazy**
by Joanna Macy and Chris Johnstone. ISBN: 978-157731972-6
This book is a much fuller explanation of the deep ecology process summarised in this chapter, plus a lot of good insights on meeting the future well.

▌ **The Dream of the Earth**
by Thomas Berry. (Various editions available)
An encouraging vision of hope arising from deep collaboration between humanity and our planet.

▌ **Relevant Networks:**
Here are websites for some of the UK organisations exploring resilience, wellbeing, and growing into the future.

www.actionforhappiness.org This is part of a large UK charity. AFH has local groups and events, also books, podcasts and other resources listed on their website.

www.networkofwellbeing.org Excellent resources on their website, and some events and local groups.

www.transitionnetwork.org Now a large international network with a lot of good approaches and many local groups and events. Also helpful books and other resources.

CONCLUSION

Chapter Twenty-One

Sunshine of Your Love: this could be so good!

DO YOU REMEMBER the sheer exuberance of the Cream song, and its passionate lyrics: *I've been waiting so long, to be where I'm going, in the sunshine of your Love...* I chose this chapter title as a reminder to find the juice here, now, in every moment. We're at the last chapter, where our shared journey ends. This could be a good chance for you to consider what you've gained from this book, and what you want from the next phases of your life ahead. This chapter offers some parting thoughts to help you.

> *We shall not cease from exploration*
> *And the end of all our exploring*
> *Will be to arrive where we started*
> *And know the place for the first time.*
> T. S. Eliot, Four Quartets

What did the 1960s mean for you?

This decade, and perhaps the early 1970s, were *the* formative years for the baby boomer generation. I suggest you revisit your own memories of those years, and also do a bit of research. The Top Hundred 45s of the 1960s will surprise you.

Can you recall the political highlights of those times? The Cuba missile crisis? Paris in May 1968? I remember feeling that anything was possible, from terminal nuclear holocaust to the collapse of the Establishment. This was a decade where the laws and culture in

Britain became far more liberal. The contraceptive pill arrived in 1961. Homosexuality was legalised in 1967. The music, the miniskirt, the drug scene, swinging London, were all statements of youthful freedom.

The key question is, what was your experience of the Sixties, and what might this mean for you now? What were your dreams, hopes, ideals, fears, for yourself and the world? Can you revive some of those young hopes, and start living them now? Remember yourself at the age of 16, 18, 21: what would the young you say to the old you?

Choose your reality

If you ask me what I've learned from nearly fifty years of adult life, this is a major insight. As we explored in Chapter 15, often our reality seems to be dictated to us: by our own repeating negative story, or by overwhelm from the media.

It takes some effort to become conscious of all this, and to realise we do have the power to choose our reality, to decide how we react even to major setbacks.

Why not take a minute to look back through the Contents page of this book? Are you aware of all the gifts and resources in your life? Have you faced the challenges? If not, try setting yourself a timescale to do this, maybe using some of the Fresh Maps and new tools this book offers.

Both habits and external pressures keep pulling us away from wellbeing, and into stress. This is why mindfulness and similar methods are so valuable: we have to keep choosing to feel the reality of this moment, in order to find the most joy in life.

How perspective helps

The poet T. S. Eliot, in *Four Quartets*, makes my point better than I can:

> *It seems, as one becomes older,*
> *That the past has another pattern, and ceases to be a*
> *mere sequence*
> *…We had the experience, but missed the meaning,*
> *And approach to the meaning restores the experience*
> *In a different form, …*

If turning seventy is a kind of watershed, looking back over your life and seeking the meaning is a helpful step. It may give you a sense of where the plotline is, of what you're still seeking, or of missing pieces in the picture, which become a goal to complete in the future. This process of finding meaning, of giving perspective, is part of the elder's role. If you do this, you're probably serving others too: your family, friends, and even strangers may learn from your insights, and be inspired to seek their own. The Self-help process below is one way to do this.

When you've done this process, notice what events were most vivid for you, and what kind of memories came up most: was it happy times or hard ones? Remember, you can change the story and choose your reality!

Self-help process 9: Timeline Insights

This exercise can help you review your life story, and gain perspective from it. You could do this in an hour, but more time would help you go deeper.

Start by guess at what age you'll die. Then calculate your whole life-span as a day or a year, and work out where key events in your life would appear in this.

(For example, if I am 69, and expect to live till 84, a year in my life equals 17 minutes in a day, and my current age is 7.42pm.
The birth of my first daughter, when I was 29, is 8.12am.

Now create a physical timeline to represent your whole life-span. You can use rope, cable, even loo roll. Mark key events into the timeline. Now, stand at the start of the line, your birth point. Try to *experience* the story of your life, walking very slowly along the line, pausing at each point where a memory comes up.

You may want to repeat all or part of the journey. Spend some time in the present moment on your line, seeking meaning for the journey so far, and picturing your hopes and intentions for the years ahead of you.

Give yourself time to reflect on this process, and write notes or a journal piece to remember what you've learned.

The road to heaven is paved with good intentions

It's a pity that intentions have got a bad name because of the old proverb. Setting positive intentions can be a powerful way of helping you make positive changes and fulfil your hopes. As you review insights from this book, from the 1960s, from your timeline, get as clear as you can about what you'd like in the years ahead. You may want qualities, like peace of mind, or specific outcomes like a new relationship or a better place to live.

Here are some pointers about setting and using intentions:

+ Be as specific and vivid as you can about what you want.
+ State your intention: say it out loud, write it up and put it on the wall, name it to someone else.
+ Consider setting a time goal, e.g. "I intend to find a new home with (specific features) within the next four months."
+ Picture yourself fulfilling the intention: see and feel this experience as vividly as you can. This gives your intention more power, and it's worth repeating this step often.
+ As you picture fulfilment, notice if doubts, fears or resistance arise. Maybe part of you believes an old story, and thinks you don't deserve things, or fears you won't sustain them.
+ If you have a spiritual path, turn your intentions into a prayer, and ask for help in realising them.

The final word – Blind Faith

We surely have to conclude with a Sixties lyric. Blind Faith formed in 1968 when Cream broke up: it included Eric Clapton, Ginger Baker, and Steve Winwood, whose voice still electrifies me. Imagine this with Eric's soaring guitar, Ginger's thumping drums, and Steve's elvish voice. The lyrics opposite are from *Sea of Joy*:

* * *

Following the shadows of the skies,
Or are they only figments of my eyes?
And I'm feeling close to when the race is run,
Waiting in our boats to set sail,
SEA OF JOY.

Self-help processes

Printed in Great Britain
by Amazon

71753411R00102